FROM
Rags
TO
RESTAURANTS

Donesa —
Thank you for
believing in me!
I am deeply grateful.

Misty

FROM **Rags** TO **RESTAURANTS**

MISTY YOUNG

The
SECRET
RECIPE

Advantage®

Published by Advantage, Charleston, South Carolina.
Member of Advantage Media Group.

ADVANTAGE is a registered trademark and the Advantage colophon is a trademark of Advantage Media Group, Inc.

Printed in the United States of America.

ISBN: 978-159932-377-0
LCCN: 2013944031

This publication is designed to provide accurate and authoritative information in regard to the subject matter covered. It is sold with the understanding that the publisher is not engaged in rendering legal, accounting, or other professional services. If legal advice or other expert assistance is required, the services of a competent professional person should be sought.

Advantage Media Group is proud to be a part of the Tree Neutral® program. Tree Neutral offsets the number of trees consumed in the production and printing of this book by taking proactive steps such as planting trees in direct proportion to the number of trees used to print books. To learn more about Tree Neutral, please visit **www.treeneutral.com**. To learn more about Advantage's commitment to being a responsible steward of the environment, please visit **www.advantagefamily.com/green**

Advantage Media Group is a publisher of business, self-improvement, and professional development books and online learning. We help entrepreneurs, business leaders, and professionals share their Stories, Passion, and Knowledge to help others Learn & Grow. Do you have a manuscript or book idea that you would like us to consider for publishing? Please visit **advantagefamily.com** or call **1.866.775.1696**.

This book is dedicated to all restaurant owners worldwide. Thank you for your kind service and your interest in improving your business.

With special thanks to my daughters, Shila Morris and Kay Young and to the best husband that ever lived: Gary Young. I deeply appreciate you all.

I am also thankful for my son in law, Chad Morris and my future son in law, Daniel Salerno, who created the custom graphics in this book.

I greatly appreciate my editorial board: Anya Lawrence, Sharon Waterhouse, Shila Morris and Kay Young. You've provided a valuable resource to independent restaurateurs everywhere. Thank you!

Finally, to every guest who has ever enjoyed a visit to the Squeeze In, or taught us how to do it better, and to every associate who gave of themselves lovingly and helped build this awesome company. Thank you!

TABLE OF CONTENTS

CHAPTER THREE | 61

ROCKET FUEL FOR RESTAURANT GROWTH: THE MAIN INGREDIENTS

CHAPTER FOUR | 83

THE FIVE IRREFUTABLE LAWS OF RESTAURANT SUCCESS

CHAPTER EIGHT I 167

DO THE RIGHT THING: SERVE ROCK STARS EVERY DAY

MODERN MARKETING: YOU DO THE MATH, BE SOCIAL!

THE SECRET RECIPE

CHAPTER ONE

Bobby Flay Shocks Me With a Throwdown!

It began with an anonymous phone call, seemingly out of the blue.

I had worked the restaurant early that day in November 2009. It was a particularly tough day. I was tired, no longer used to working the floor after so many years of my restaurant experience. I finally sat down to do my regular job, administrative tasks, systems review financials, e-mail, organize the office, all the background things restaurateurs do to keep business going smoothly. Nothing glamorous.

In the middle of my quiet concentration time the phone rings. The voice on the phone is direct, to the point: "Hi, I'm calling to ask some questions about omelettes." That's the thing my restaurant, the Squeeze In, is known for: fabulous omelettes. This

> That's the thing my restaurant, the Squeeze In, is known for: fabulous omelettes.

lady sets me up, spends an hour with me, asking all kinds of questions about our omelettes, recipes, and restaurants, and about my family. Having spent nearly two decades in public and media relations, I naturally assumed from the nature of her questioning she was with a media outlet, but I didn't at all expect to hear her say, "I'm with the Food Network."

THE FOOD NETWORK

A call from the Food Network is nearly every restaurateur's dream. How was I going to contain myself? I was stoked beyond belief and yet totally freaked out at the same time. The woman said that within an hour of the end of the phone call I needed to send additional material for her decision. There was absolutely only one answer to that: "Sure!"

And one final thing she also asked. "Would you please create a little seven-minute casting video and have it on my desk in New York City first thing Monday morning?"

This was a Thursday afternoon. She wanted the video on her desk across the country in four days. She gave me very specific instructions on what to include. It meant we'd have to shoot, edit, package, and ship within 48 hours.

"Sure. No problem," I repeated. "We can have that to you early Monday morning," thinking, "Oh my gosh, today's Thursday." I know another restaurateur might have hesitated, asked for more time, thinking New York is needlessly in a hurry. But we got it done. It was intense. We filmed the next morning, Friday. We edited Saturday and that very afternoon delivered the video to FedEx, and it was on her desk in New York City on deadline. That seven-minute video helped set amazing things in motion.

Little did we know 13 months later we would be filming an episode of *Throwdown! with Bobby Flay*, one of the most recognized cooking shows on national television at the time.

But before we met Bobby, there was a lengthy quiet period, months and months of complete silence from the Food Network until we received another call.

It was a different person this time, but an interesting, intriguing, question. "Will you and the family be around in the fall?" this woman asked.

"Yes, we will," I said. Even though we had been thinking about taking a trip, we would definitely be in town.

"Great! The Food Network has selected the Squeeze In to be part of a Valentine's Day special, *For the Love of Food*. There are three restaurants included, one each for breakfast, lunch, and dinner. You'll be the breakfast part," she said.

They took us down that whole path of a Valentine's Day special because that's how they did the *Throwdown! with Bobby Flay*.

It's a setup. They don't tell you it's Bobby Flay; that'd ruin the whole surprise, right? After the show aired, I had so many people ask me, "Did you know? You had to know!" But the absolute truth is *no, we didn't know*. We had been filming, starting at the Truckee location and then at our home, and the final day, in our Reno restaurant, which was packed with some of our most loyal guests who wanted to help and be a part of the Valentine's Day show on an insanely cold, snowy morning. During that time there was no wink, no nod, no grin, no glance, no nothing from the producer, director, photographers, or sound crew that indicated it was anything other than a Food Network Valentine's Day special.

BOBBY FLAY COMES IN FROM THE COLD

That is, until the moment Bobby Flay came in from the blizzard, walking into my restaurant in Reno, Nevada, in the middle of this "Food Network Valentine's Day Love-In" we were hosting for our guests. After weaving his way to the front of the crowd, Bobby Flay stood front and center. My daughter and business partner, Shila Morris, who saw Bobby before I did, said, "I think there's a question in the front row." I turned and was completely flabbergasted to see him standing there and just started shouting, "No! No! Oh my God! Bobby Flay!" He is one of the world's most recognized celebrity chefs, and

> I turned and was completely flabbergasted to see him standing there and just started shouting, "No! No! Oh my God! Bobby Flay!" He is one of the world's most recognized celebrity chefs, and here he is standing in my restaurant, the one I had led from struggle to success.

here he is standing in my restaurant, the one I had led from struggle to success.

I thought I might barf right then and there from the stress of the moment, but I remember thinking, "It's not a good idea to puke on national TV." I wasn't going to hurl. I can compose myself in the most trying of times—but I did flap my wrists like an exuberant toddler. I looked a little crazy, but that's what happened. You can see the episode on our website at www.squeezein.com.

With Bobby Flay standing there, it was clear this wasn't going to be *For the Love of Food*. He was there for a *Throwdown!*

As Bobby looked around, scanning the faces of my blizzard-chapped guests, Shila said, "We're ready for a *Throwdown!*" Without missing a beat, Bobby replied, "Who said anything about a *Throwdown!?* I'm doing some research on snow cones; I'm here for a *snow*down!" It was pretty funny.

After the laughter and fun banter, we got right to it. We spent the next couple of hours preparing omelettes and trying each other's dishes and having the guests testing and tasting and enjoying the food. As a funny side note, the omelette we served to Bobby at the Squeeze In was the first omelette ever made by Shila. Very cool.

AND THE WINNERS ARE ...

When the judges voted, Bobby Flay won.

I was a good sport about it of course, but an hour later when the cameras were no longer around, I found myself in the vacant office suite next door, bawling my eyes out, being comforted and consoled by Shila and my husband, Gary. Yet because I come from a place of gratitude in life and in business, I was thrilled for the opportunity that had just happened and said so on the program to Bobby. Still, it was the sense of loss, on national TV, that was getting to me.

Comforting me, Gary said, "You know what? It's all good. We have so much to be thankful for! We'll be featured on the Food Network, on *Throwdown! with Bobby Flay*. You know who really won the *Throwdown!?* We all did. It was a successful episode for Bobby Flay, the Food Network, the Squeeze In, and for our family." And Shila added, "Thank you, Mom, for being the leader of our family and our company. We're thankful you had us ready for this, thankful for the opportunity!" They were reiterating back to me what I'd hammered on for years: "Anything is possible; we have to be ready." In time, I learned that while we didn't win the cooking contest, we surely didn't lose.

> It was a successful episode for Bobby Flay, the Food Network, the Squeeze In, and for our family.

I found that Gary and Shila were absolutely right. Immediately after the show aired—literally, *the very next morning*—our business got a 25 percent boost. We began to see guests from all over the country and the world. People from out of state would take cab rides from casinos to come try our omelettes.

We've since opened a third location, and now a fourth, faster than we had originally planned, and we're looking toward continued growth for the Squeeze In family of restaurants. I'd say the exposure and resultant credibility moved our business plan forward by five years. Bobby Flay gave us so much to be thankful for.

Our so-called "loss" on *Throwdown! with Bobby Flay* on national television? It was actually a win: it attracted more word of mouth and exposure. Losing was winning. The fact that Bobby came to meet me? I was seen as good enough for Bobby to want to challenge me in what my restaurant does best: omelettes. More than once during the show Bobby said, "Misty, you are the nicest competitor in *Throwdown!* history." That's part of who I am: *I believe kindness and courtesy matter.*

It was no accident that we got the attention of the Food Network. We attracted it because we were doing all the right things out front in our business: great food and service, happy guests and associates *and* behind-the-scenes work to get noticed. In fact, in that original first phone call, I asked the Food Network producer, "How did you find us? What made you call us?"

Her answer?

"Well, we troll the Internet and we listen to what people are saying and then we go take a look. We check out potential opportunities. We search, then scout."

Ultimately we had been preparing for this moment for years. We were ready.

PREPPING FOR SUCCESS

That's how they found us. But let's go back in time and take a look at what came before the Food Network's November phone call. This was no random Yellow Pages search for omelettes.

What had I been doing up to that point? Developing systems, working with people and ideas, being creative. At the Squeeze In we had an up-to-date website without typos. It was complete with photos, videos, our menu, vibrant colors, media mentions and links, and meaningful, relevant information for our guests. Not just on our website either but on our Facebook page, Flickr account, and YouTube. As far back as 2006 we were actively using social media tools to strategically convey our brand and personality. All of that paid off in attracting the Food Network and *Throwdown! with Bobby Flay.*

What does this tell me when I look back at the Food Network and Bobby Flay standing in my restaurant?

The work we had all been doing until that point was sound strategy. We were reaching our goals and had largely succeeded while emphasizing how much more there was to do.

Any time restaurant owners hear the words, "The Food Network," on the other end of the phone,

> What does this tell me when I look back at the Food Network and Bobby Flay standing in my restaurant?

they realize this could be the big time. It doesn't get much bigger than the Food Network in terms of media opportunities in the restaurant business, and it absolutely doesn't get bigger than Bobby Flay in terms of Food Network superstars.

Having the opportunity to do the *Throwdown!* with him and realizing the Food Network can have its pick out of hundreds of thousands of independent restaurants across the country and that it picked us was huge. It set us apart. And as for our local market, this is where it really hit home. We were only the second *Throwdown!* episode to be featured in the entire state of Nevada.

As of this writing, 103 episodes of *Throwdown! with Bobby Flay* have been produced and ours was one of them. It's a huge

> We were only the second *Throwdown!* episode to be featured in the entire state of Nevada.

opportunity and an amazing honor just to be considered, *let alone featured.*

That's all good news. But if you were to look at the day our family took ownership of the Squeeze, you would never in a million years have guessed it could be featured on the Food Network, or that I would become a restaurateur known on national television—and a coach, consultant, and industry expert speaker. I now have the amazing opportunity to help others live their dream and hack (which I define as smart, fast-track, cut-the-crap-learning) into success. This book will share the secret recipe to restaurant success through our unlikely rags-to-restaurants story.

Running a restaurant is both an art and a science, and we'll look carefully at both aspects.

TURN BACK THE CLOCK TO OUR FIRST DAY

December 28, 2003, my first day of work at the Squeeze. A raging blizzard. That very morning, as I got ready at home in Reno to drive 30 miles up Interstate 80 to Truckee, California, nestled in the cradle of the High Sierra, it was snowing sideways in both towns, and all along the I-80 corridor.

Walking out to get into the truck at 5:30 on that dark morning, I slipped on the ice and fell face first toward the asphalt. Somehow my fist caught me right in the center of my chest and saved my face from smashing the pavement. The wind was knocked out of me but not out of my sails, I lay there for a couple seconds, assessing if I'd been badly hurt. I ended up with only a beautiful bruise right over my heart.

Not so auspicious, but I warmly regard that bruise as my original "love tattoo" for the Squeeze In, and it's been a lovefest ever since. Sometimes love hurts, right?

We had initially decided that Gary would stay at his salaried position as a landscape construction foreman while I worked with the Squeeze. So that morning I left alone. As I arrived at the Squeeze to take over ownership, I was fully on fire, passionate, and alive, and I couldn't wait to dig in. I was absolutely in love with the Squeeze and wanted to care for, nurture, and gaze adoringly at my new lover (you totally know how that feels!).

It was this tiny, cool, old-school, hippie-style restaurant with one small bank of windows, long-overdue-to-be-refinished hardwood floors and a whole lot of work to be done. It was just 10' 3" wide and 62' deep. The walls were covered in signatures, drawings, and eye candy galore. With only 12 tables, seating 49, guests had to squeeze in, and often, different parties were seated together "family style" to maximize the limited space. The gentleman we had purchased it from, Jerry Bussell, said, "You'll have to work it, hands on. It needs you to be there."

That day, I walked into a well-loved restaurant patronized by tens of thousands of people, but, as Jerry had warned us, it had some problems. It had service issues, and consistency and cash management issues. It needed some serious upgrades. It needed love. It needed systems. And Jerry was right: *it needed the owners to be there.*

I walked in fired up, ready to go, and energized to bring this business into the modern era. It was created in the 1970s and it had stayed '70s style until 2004 when we started upgrades to bring it into the twenty-first century.

We had to implement modern systems in every category from physical plant to people to products. It's crazy to think there was not an actual business telephone in the restaurant for incoming calls. When a guest called the listed telephone number, a payphone in the hallway would ring. In the middle of serving guests or cleaning tables, a waitress would have to run from the restaurant floor to the hallway and answer the payphone!

There was an access hole cut through the wall of the kitchen right on the other side of the payphone so that the cooks could reach over and answer too if necessary. That was just crazy, like something from a comedy, only it was my new life. I relished it.

The Squeeze didn't take credit cards—cash only. There was no fax machine. There was no soda fountain system—sodas were still served in cans—no recipes, no portion control, no waste sheets, no organized system for ordering, receiving, or inventory.

There were limited systems to gauge success and hold folks accountable. There was no system to monitor and record handwritten guest checks. In a 100 percent cash restaurant handwritten tickets are not a good scenario, not a good way to help keep honest people honest. There was no point-of-sale system, no reports, no job descriptions, no manuals or handbooks.

Yes, of course, as far as I could tell, given the lack of accountability (and my lack of experience in financial management), the servers and server/manager did a good job with the deposits and daily sales information, and so on. But with zero systems, it was clear the business was technologically behind the times and needed swift action. I let the managing bookkeeper go on day 11 and took on all her duties myself. She had been there for 26 years and it was quite clear she wasn't part of the solution.

Yet, for all the lack of systems, the Squeeze had a tremendous amount going for it. The place was supercool. You could literally feel the "love vibe" in there. It had a total 1970s, keep-on-trucking kind of look to it. Even the logo looked like a 1970s T-shirt, which we decided not to change much. The old-man-in-the-moon logo had this sort of grumpy look, his lips blowing out a smoky stream of stars. We upgraded the grumpy old man to a smiley man in the moon, fresh new stars streaming out of his mouth, which better suited our style.

We were going to project a more modern image with the upgraded logo: the same, but happier. The logo was of course just one tiny part of it, as there were many strategic improvements in our near future.

TRUCKEE, CALIFORNIA

SURPRISE REPAIRS

This awesome little 30-year-old restaurant was in need of some basic cleaning and upgrades. But some repairs came to us as a complete surprise, like the entire heating system, which died—on day four.

The death of the heater nearly shut us down, not just because it was deep winter with single-digit temperatures, but because I called the fire department across the street and said, "Gee, it smells like natural gas in here and the heater's not working." The fire chief walked over and red-tagged us, saying, "You've got to get that fixed immediately or you'll be closed." When I called the landlord and explained the situation, there was another surprise awaiting me. "Well, you've got a triple net lease and that's your responsibility," he told me. "Hire a contractor."

Yes, this was my dream, but here we were just four days in, already with a $5,000 cash expense. It was little things such as the payphone and no fax all the way up to giant things such as replacing the heating system that were among the many challenges we had to overcome.

Add to that the lack of systems and internal account-ability. At the end of the day, all the cash was recorded and bundled up and put into plastic bread baggies and dropped into a hidden safe. Once a week or so, someone would pull the money out of the safe and make a deposit. Obviously, that was one of the first systems we upgraded, both through daily deposits and by accepting credit cards to reduce the overall amount of cash on hand. Credit cards also helped boost sales, as guests began spending more with cards.

I remember when we would drive up for breakfast from Reno, before we bought the place, and half way up the hill, one of us would say, "Oh man, did anybody bring cash? They don't take cards. I always forget." We'd stop at an ATM or grocery store to get cash. Accepting credit cards was a huge change for the restaurant. And just that one tiny thing helped modernize the Squeeze, a decades-ahead jump in one little step, solidly bringing the Squeeze into the twenty-first century.

BEING FOUND IN THE DIGITAL AGE

I think about the Food Network producer saying, "We troll the Internet …" and I'm so thankful. As soon as we bought the Squeeze In and began to develop systems, I started thinking about the most basic marketing: a website. I had come from a marketing background and my immediate thought was, "I wonder if the domain name is available?" I knew we didn't have a website, but I wondered if the name Squeeze In was already gone.

This was 2004. I thought, of course, the domain name www.squeezein.com had to be taken; there was no way it was available. Shock of shocks. It was available, and I grabbed it on the spot. Once the domain name was secured, I immediately began to draw up a basic website and hired a developer.

We've had a good (and constantly refining) web presence ever since, which we are always upgrading and updating regularly. In today's business world, particularly, as Web 2.0—the interactive, social web—has developed, you have to have a good profile, starting with a good website—and today, a mobile website at minimum. These are basic components of helping your guests and potential guests find you. If you don't go mobile, your potential guest's fingers aren't the only thing that will do the walking!

> In today's business world, particularly, as Web 2.0–the interactive, social web–has developed, you have to have a good profile, starting with a good website.

Your website has to work with smartphones, tablets, and other mobile devices people may be using in their cars or on the street walking through a city, trying to find you. It's got to have your menu and hours, basic information about the restaurant, and a button someone with big fingers can push once to call you right now. And your address. You'd be amazed how many brick and mortar businesses don't make their physical address easy to find on a website. Those are just the bare minimums.

In 2006 I set up our YouTube and Myspace pages (yes, Myspace!), and in 2008, a Facebook page. But we didn't initially do social media well. We did what's known as a "post and ghost." We set it up and walked away. Not a strategic move.

A year later we had 224 Facebook followers having a lovely conversation about us, but not with us, and without any promotion or participation on our end. That first year we had done very little with it.

When I realized those 224 people were talking *about* us and not *with* us, I said, "My goal is to get 10,000 fans on this Facebook page in a year." I thought it would be easy. Well, it hasn't been. In spring 2013, between a main brand page and individual restaurant location pages (for "check-ins"), we had nearly 8,000 fans. We now understand better how to grow the base, and how to be relevant and engaging. And we pay attention to constant changes being made by Facebook to continue leveraging and building our base.

A smart starting point in today's economy: *People have to be able to find you and you've got to meet people where they are—* on phones, laptops, tablets, smart watches, through Google Glass. The channels grow constantly. Guests and potential guests are in their car, at the gym, at their desk, at charitable events. Author of the book *Become Your Own Boss in 12 Months* and *New York Times* social media blogger Melinda Emerson, known as @SmallBizLady on Twitter, said, "Social media is the best thing that ever happened to small business!" Most social tools are free and all are fairly easy to use.

Yet restaurants must be proactive in the social space. It doesn't mean you have to do *everything*. In fact, I strongly believe *social tools must be used as much as necessary and as little as possible*. Social is where you proactively listen, post content, and seek to attract and engage guests and potential guests, but don't get consumed by it. It can seem overwhelming, and we'll discuss this in detail in a later chapter.

EXTREME LOYALTY AND BEING READY

One way we've ensured the Squeeze's continued success is through the EggHead Breakfast Club, the crown jewel of our marketing. It is our house list, our database. Squeeze guests opt in to the fully customized program, an exclusive and sophisticated points-based, loyalty- and reward-driven system.

When Squeeze guests become card-carrying EggHeads, they become members of our restaurant family. We nurture and feed them extra food, bonus points, fantastic hookups such as discounts and exclusive opportunities, invitations to VIP parties, and special, customized, members-only offers. Our loyal EggHeads act as ambassadors of our brand and family. They're part of what we call the Squeeze In lovefest. According to American Express's *Restaurant Briefing*,

> Loyal customers spend more (a recent study from the Center for Retail Management found that 12%-15% of a business' most loyal customers contribute 55%-70% of sales, consistent with similar research) and they cost less than finding new ones. In addition, loyal customers are highly likely to recommend a restaurant to others—a recent study by Granbury Restaurant Solutions

found that 82% of restaurant loyalty program members referred at least one person, while 42% referred four or more.

As of spring 2013 we've attracted over 63,215 individual members into the program. What does that mean for a small business like ours? It means that we're not at the mercy of traditional, institutional, old-school, image advertising. In today's world there are three types of media: owned, earned, and paid. Andrews Nachison, founder of We Media, said, "Institutions that once had to go through media to deliver information *are now themselves media.*"

At the Squeeze In, we are the media. We own the media. We use direct-response media methods. We are a proactive, forward-moving business and all four of our restaurants offer this modern opt-in system of outreach and development to a whole herd of people who want to be part of what we have going on. Wouldn't you like to have that too? I'll introduce you fully to our program soon.

It is incredibly powerful for a restaurant to have guests voluntarily share their names, addresses, phone numbers, e-mails, birth and anniversary dates, home and cell-phone numbers, and information about kids in the household. All of this helps in developing and designing meaningful, relevant rewards, and marketing promotions. It allows the restaurant to follow up with surveys making sure all the right things are being done to market the company and serve the guests. Best of all? Guests love it. They love giving the information that makes the restaurant better at serving their needs while at the same time helping the restaurant to grow exponentially.

FOOD NETWORK QUESTIONS HAVE ANSWERS

The depth of information and detail available through the EggHead Breakfast Club and our integrated point-of-sale system were major reasons why we were so on the ball when the Food Network made that initial call to us, seemingly out of the blue.

Before our many upgrades such as the EggHead Breakfast Club and the point-of-sale system, when we first started out, I think if the Food Network had chanced upon us, we would not have made the cut. We didn't have our act together. We weren't yet well organized. We hadn't developed great systems, and surely at that time we wouldn't have been able to say, "We're going to serve our three thousandth Racy Tracy Omelette soon." However, because we had developed, used, and continued to refine our systems, I had the information and the credibility to deliver that kind of statement when the Food Network called.

That was part of what the Food Network found so valuable about us. We knew our numbers. We were able to say to them, "Yes, we serve X number of eggs. We serve X number of meals. We serve X number of guests on a daily, weekly, annual basis." I delivered those numbers the first time they called and many more via e-mail by that afternoon's first deadline! Not five days later, not five weeks later, but that November day of the very first phone call. Numbers are real. Measurements are real. *Facts are valuable tools in your business and you get to them through systems.*

Accurate numbers and reporting are the fundamental management tools needed to succeed in the restaurant business. That's not a secret!

Had we not had in place our background, our foundation, our systems, our numbers, our website, and all of the tools that make a business strong, we never would have had the opportunity to begin with. The Food Network might have sent in its scouts and said, "Oh they have a cute little restaurant here. Too bad they're not ready to go. Too bad they're not ready for prime time."

The fundamentals and accurate, reliable numbers helped us expand. But Gary and I didn't get to a second location alone. Although, back in 2003, we cashed in retirements and scraped together everything we had to buy the Squeeze, we made a critical and strategic decision in 2006 that changed everything: we brought on partners.

BRINGING ON PARTNERS

Most times, I think it's probably not a great idea to bring on partners, but in this case, it made sense. We carefully selected our partners not for their money but for their youthful energy and commitment to our company. We picked our daughter and son-in-law, Shila and Chad Morris. The Morrises didn't buy in with cash. Rather, they've purchased their shares in labor, love, and longevity. Today they run all operations as the true day-to-day leadership of the company.

Shila is the president of the Squeeze In and Chad is her vice president. I serve as chair of the board and chief strategist, while Gary, our human battery, is the ultimate support of all of us. Each one of us brings a complementary and valuable skill to the company, and we make a great team. We are blessed to work together as a family.

For us, the two roads of opportunity and preparation converged. We did all the strategic planning to prepare, building our website, creating consistent products and service, building our loyalty program, designing, implementing, and continuously refining systems. Preparation has its own gravitational pull. Success is about taking action!

> Preparation has its own gravitational pull. Success is about taking action!

I've heard it said that "reasons precede results." The following chapter is all about our many reasons to strive for results.

FINDING TRUE LOVE

That was back in 1979, the same year that I, at the tender age of 17, met my handsome SoCal surfer dude, Gary Young. I found in him the 21-year-old man of my dreams. He was kind, fun, loving, compassionate, hysterically funny, and had a ton of energy and ideas. His college-educated, never-divorced folks had been married for nearly 40 years and all five kids in his family were from the same parents and had lived in one house for a very long time. It was like stepping into a family from a black and white photograph. They lovingly accepted me, although I was a bit wary of their long stability. Even though I had always wanted that in my own life, it seemed unachievable and odd.

At the time we met, Gary and I had exactly 83 cents, a half tank of gas in Gary's 1964 black Volkswagen, covered with surf stickers and a pack of ciggies (we quit decades ago) and a whole lot of love and fun. We turned in soda bottles at the grocery store for a nickel apiece to scrape up enough cash for gas or smokes. Because I was 17, California required us to get approval from a judge to get married. Mom and the judge signed off, and Gary and I set about wedding planning.

Six months later, we held a simple wedding in a mountain meadow in Mt. Baldy, California. Some 150 people, and several dogs decorated with ribbons and bows, trekked down a long rocky trail to the ceremony spot. That evening's reception at the Mt. Baldy Lodge was filled with laughter, dancing, one six-foot-long sandwich, and an incredibly beautiful six-layer rainbow cake made and decorated by my talented mother. The whole event cost $200, including handmade invitations, wedding dress, tuxedo, and dance band. Gary and I were both a little put off later as we heard about the betting—people were actually betting against us. I suppose a 17-year-old bride and a just-turned-22-year-old groom don't often succeed for the long haul. I don't think our wedding guests realized how truly in love we were. Now, we're on the verge of our third grandchild and more in love than ever, with the maturity of decades and daily commitment to our relationship.

Still, it was uphill from the start. We'd been living in a tiny Mt. Baldy cabin. After the wedding, we moved many of our things, including wedding presents, into a larger cabin the night before we moved our bed. Gary said he didn't think it was a good idea. I was insistent it was fine. By the next morning, the cabin had been broken into, and many of our wedding presents had been ripped off. I've appreciated and respected the value of Gary's wisdom ever since.

Our old VW broke down 500 miles from home on our campout honeymoon. We didn't care; it was "just vapor lock," so we sat on the interstate until the motor cooled and we could drive again. Our jobs paid minimum wage and money was supertight. When we moved from Mt. Baldy down into "the city," it was to a studio in a rough neighborhood in Ontario, California, directly under the flight path at the end of the Ontario International Airport runway. Those were difficult days. The neighborhood was loud with jets, fights, guns, tires peeling, and women screaming. Scary times, but being together made it bearable.

THE LEARNING PATH

I was fortunate to be accepted into a state-funded, job-training program, the California Employment and Training Act (CETA), designed to assist low-income people. I was monetarily poor, yes, but I was also emotionally poor. I had been pushed around and ridiculed from school to school. Picked on continuously, I had little self-esteem. I embraced and rigorously studied the curriculum of human potential and upward mobility (that's where I got "the bug"), took every personality and career/vocation test known to psychologists, attended group workshops and counseling, and ironically got assigned as a teaching aide to the Mt. Baldy Elementary

School, attended by my own siblings. It was a great fit as I learned to love learning—and teaching—and began to find value in myself. While Gary and I were poor, we were never impoverished. We believed in each other and our ultimate ability to succeed. Sometimes love really is all you need.

I started reading many books on my own. David Schwartz's *The Magic of Thinking Big* became my Bible as I began to seriously dream of a life I had never previously considered.

We were very thankful for Gary's folks, Wesley and Lila Young, who often stopped by with bags of groceries, cleaning supplies, and a bit of cash to help out.

When Wes won the job of his dreams to teach criminal justice 500 miles away at the University of Nevada, Reno, he leaped at the opportunity. Tragically, six months later, Wes was diagnosed with cancer and died soon after, leaving Lila alone in Nevada. Gary and I just looked at each other and said, "You know, maybe we could go be helpful to Mom, and we could get a new start at the same time." We had a giant garage sale, gave everything else to Goodwill and drove the 500 miles to Reno. We both knew two people: each other and Lila, who quickly became my second-closest friend.

CETA had inspired in me a thirst for learning, but possibly more importantly, helped me develop self-belief, the idea that I was actually capable and had potential. I had already exited Claremont High School early when my guidance counselor called me in and said, "You passed the California High-School Proficiency Exam." I had taken the test at age 15 but was a junior at the time. When I was 16,

Mr. Sargent said I was free to go. I cleaned out my locker and walked that very morning. I was sick of being bullied and somehow knew I had something in me bigger than high school. Although my GPA was only 1.96 (hey, it's a strong D, after all!), upon arriving in Nevada, it was time to fulfill my dream of going to college, and I began classes at the University of Nevada, Reno.

Ultimately, the university challenged my residency, and I had to drop out. Only living in Nevada a short time, I couldn't substantiate residency and couldn't afford the non-resident tuition. It was a blessing anyway. I strangely hadn't been feeling well, had been fuzzy, unable to focus with difficulty concentrating, all completely foreign to me. After almost six years of marriage, I discovered I was pregnant.

A GROWING FAMILY

Gary worked full time for a landscape company in the summer and drove a heating fuel delivery truck in the wintertime. I became a VISTA (Volunteers in Service to America) for the Salvation Army. Even so, we weren't able to make it without help. With a baby on the way, we qualified to stand in line for commodities: government butter, cheese, and even chunky Department of Agriculture chicken or beef in a big tin can. Gelatinous government chicken is funky in tacos, spaghetti, or stir-fry, but government food got us through difficult times. I'm thankful for the assistance, even if it's tough to talk about those days.

Baby Shila was born at home without complications the summer of 1985. At the Salvation Army's Family Emergency Shelter, I was making friends with colleagues and doing good works. We were on food stamps and WIC (Women, Infants, Children) and the Salvation Army often helped us stock our pantry while boosting our joy. We were truly paupers, but we were happy, always striving, always looking forward, believing against the wedding oddsmakers, against the odds themselves, that we would make it somehow.

Although we were super appreciative of the assistance, it was embarrassing to be on food stamps and WIC. In those days WIC checks were oversized, obvious, blue-green, 9" x 4" vouchers. Discretion wasn't an option. Half the time the cashier would make a big deal: "You can't use your WIC coupon on the 21.2 ounce package." Up comes the microphone. "I need a 16.4-ounce box of Kix Cereal on check stand seven," complete with eye rolling and impatient huffing by the clerk and the other folks in line.

When we displayed the blatant WIC voucher and unmistakable food stamps ticket book at the cash register, everyone knew we were on public assistance. We might as well have publically announced, "We're on welfare!" It was difficult to substantiate my growing personal belief of having something to offer, of being able to become someone of value to others when, for years, I was the new kid, pushed around, different, undeniably poor, wearing hand-me-downs and shoes with holes, my self-esteem only blooming as an adult, and then to be frequently reminded that I was still poor and worthless.

We struggled through those difficult, early, family years, as most folks do on the road to self-improvement and providing a better life for their families. Looking back, I see both how little—*and how much*—we had—evenings of playing board games, working jigsaw puzzles, dance parties to the loud radio. With the kind help of Lila, providing a small down payment for a fixer-upper house, we had finally been able to purchase a starter home, which, of course, came with new responsibilities, expenses, and duties.

These were tough days. We still lived just outside the ghetto, heard regular gunfire and breaking windows and sirens, and that was our life, and we were happy. Shila was only allowed to play in the fenced backyard and couldn't walk alone to the neighborhood park a block away. Our old car broke down frequently, often leaving me stranded with a little girl in the city. We had no health insurance and still shopped at thrift stores for clothes, shoes, furniture, and appliances. Those were the Top Ramen, Lucky Charms, and hot dog days. I obsessed continuously, "How am I ever going to get out of this? What am I going to do to better myself and my family? How can I change this situation?" I had to try again to go to college. Not everyone has to go to college. There are many ways to do things right, but college was the right thing for me.

I applied again at the university. This time, three years later, residency was no problem and initially, grants and loans, and later, scholarships, helped me through the five years it took to earn a bachelor's degree in social psychology. While I attended all the classes and only my name is on the degree, I didn't earn it alone. Gary listened to and advised on every single paper, presentation, and report. My younger sister, Heidi, came to live with us to be our nanny as second baby Kay arrived just five weeks before the start of my senior year. Gary was my husband, Heidi was my wife, and it took this whole village to raise a business leader.

Those were hectic days: full-time school, working 30 hours a week, Gary, Misty, Shila, baby Kay, sister/wife Heidi and her two-year-old son, my nephew, Tony, living together in our little house, usually with at least one dog, a bird or two, and sometimes a cat and kittens.

I look back fondly remembering books and tests, papers and presentations, cooking, dancing, playing, struggling, two little girls, a little boy, and three stressed-out young adults. We made it through on autopilot. This whole family gathered to support me as I achieved the dean's list while studying sociology and psychology, Japanese, geography, astronomy, English, math and history—and could not have succeeded without them. Ah, the simple days. That was when we began to visit the Squeeze In. Those were the days of eagerly looking into the future with desire, love, and gratitude. While struggling, I always believed I had something bigger in me, something to offer, a way to serve, a way to make a meaningful difference.

In *Think and Grow Rich*, Napoleon Hill says, "Desire backed by faith knows no such word as impossible." I kept focused on a better future for us.

After graduating from college and spending 11 years in the edge-of-the-ghetto house, we began an upward migration to better living and safer neighborhoods. Gary found a two-story house with an expansive view. He kept it private for two months as he drove by and scoped it out numerous times. Finally, he took me by. I was immediately thrilled with the idea.

A BIGGER VIEW

Seeing how elegant and safe and big it was, I thought, "There's just no way we can afford it" and, of course, I didn't think we deserved it. After a couple weeks of obsessing over the house, I said, "What's it going to take? The answer's 'No' unless we ask, right? So we made an offer. We got the house with clean white walls and carpet, brand-new appliances, and nary an improvement to be made. Shocked and amazed, and with exceptional gratitude, we moved into the elegant house on the hill in a safe, quiet neighborhood, featuring a long and wide view of the gorgeous Reno valley and colorfully lighted skyline. It seemed a galaxy away from the poor neighborhood where we'd just spent well over a decade.

For me, the shift was instant. My mind immediately opened. I was no longer straddling the ghetto, with helicopters and cop cars, people running down the middle of the street carrying couches, police knocking at the door with pictures of murdered children, beat-up, bloody guys banging at the front door in the middle of the night begging for help (true story! We did, of course, help the guy, but we were terrified). I began to see new potential. I began to envision a bigger reality, a new me, new possibilities.

Up on the hill, in this new environment, I bloomed. I literally had new vision. I could physically see the entire valley and everything in between—the whole physical expanse. I drew pictures of the sky in my journal. I had never drawn pictures before. In the distance, I watched jets take off and land at the Reno-Tahoe International Airport, and, with binoculars, I could see the tire smoke on the runway. While I watched the sunrise every morning, *my internal view, my thinking, expanded to meet this new field of vision.* I was able to see much bigger opportunities for myself and my family just by changing my physical position. Jim Kwik of Kwik Learning says, "Your physiology affects your psychology." If you want to change, sometimes you just have to move—take a hike or a drive, hit the stairs or the treadmill. Sometimes you move to a new house. That's exactly what happened for me.

> If you want to change, sometimes you just have to move–take a hike or a drive, hit the stairs or the treadmill. Sometimes you move to a new house. That's exactly what happened for me.

THE ROAD TO THE RESTAURANT

Before the elegant house, while living on the edge of the ghetto and before going back to school, I had applied for a program assistant job at the YWCA, literally walking distance from home. Three-year-old Shila was enrolled in the Y preschool so this would have been a very convenient job. The newspaper advertised "Administrative Assistant: Support programs, plan events with supervision. College degree preferred, $1,300 a month."

A salary of $1,300 a month was pretty good money. I applied for, interviewed twice, and got the position. I was stoked! Immediately after they hired me, they said, "Now, because you don't have a college degree, we're only going to pay you $1,000 a month." I was crushed. I thought, "How could you do that to me? I was obviously the best candidate for the job, but you're discounting me 30 percent because I don't have a freaking piece of paper?" I didn't really need any more motivation for college, but this experience was definitely a confirmation.

I've been blessed with a great deal of energy in my life. While working at the Y and starting college, I also volunteered for a U.S. Senate campaign. Nevada's governor, Richard Bryan, was running for the U.S. Senate against an incumbent. I had no idea that 98 percent of the time an incumbent is retained and only 2 percent of challengers win. I was naïve. I didn't know that. I just thought, "Oh, I met the governor once and he was cool and I'd like to volunteer."

Within a week of volunteering on the campaign, I was offered a paid position. Bye bye YWCA and the discounted salary.

I knew, come November, win or lose, I was going to need a job. So, I secured a waitressing job to start right after the election because that was what I knew how to do. I prepaid the uniform deposit and everything. My mom had always said, "Honey, as long as you can count back change, you can get a job anywhere and you can earn a good living as a waitress."

Albert Einstein said, "Nothing happens until something moves." One thing I did well was take action, often times risks be damned, though that strategy hasn't always paid off. It has, however, made for some interesting conversations with my wonderful risk-averse husband, Gary.

As it turned out, the governor, against all the odds, unseated the incumbent U.S. senator and appointed me at his state headquarters in Reno—fantastic and totally unexpected, an unintended consequence of volunteering, of taking action. Sure made a believer out of Gary!

My interest and my action launched me. I just wanted to volunteer. I wasn't seeking anything else. I was willing to do it because I'd get a chance to do something new and exciting, learn more, and meet interesting people. Then it unexpectedly presented a career opportunity.

I worked for the senator all through college and beyond for a couple more years. Six years later, in 1994, when the senator came up for re-election, I was offered to district-manage his campaign, and I gladly accepted. During the campaign, I met and campaigned with Nevada attorney general Frankie Sue Del Papa, also running for re-election, and we got along famously. She was amazing. Frankie Sue was high energy, highly intelligent and respected, an awesome role model. She also won her race.

LESSONS FROM POLITICS

Shortly after the senator's exciting, successful re-election campaign was over, I was back to work in the day-to-day grind of the senate office and the phone rang. It was Frankie Sue, and I was simply expecting her to ask for the senator.

Instead, she told me, "I really like the energy I saw out there on the campaign trail. I think you'd make a great press secretary."

Silent for a moment, I was stunned and immediately thrilled with the prospect. I said, "I don't know how to be a press secretary, Frankie Sue." And she said, "I'll teach you." And she did.

I had no idea that I was going to become a press secretary, but I was open to it, whatever showed up. But first, I had to ask the senator, telling him, "Senator, I have this opportunity. Frankie Sue called me," and I just explained the whole situation to him. He said, "Misty you have to do it. This is an opportunity of a lifetime. You've simply got to do it." And I did. Another unintended consequence. Another huge, unanticipated result of taking action!

Frankie Sue encouraged me to run for statewide-at-large delegate to the 1996 Democratic National Convention. She told me the experience of the campaign, and if I won, attending the convention itself, would be fun.

I ran, and lo and behold, I was elected. The 1996 convention in Chicago was an amazing experience. To be part of that kind of high energy, to see the process, the politics, live and in person, was a blast. The fun, the perks, the prestige. The people I met and partied with: Tipper Gore, Kevin Costner, Dr. Ruth Westheimer, Herbie Hancock, Billy Ray Cyrus—too many names to remember! It was fantastic. It happened because I was in love with taking action. I loved the adrenaline of taking action. I still do.

Politics taught me how to get along with a tremendous variety of people, to better understand their position regardless of affiliation, and that is something I've kept at the forefront of my thinking.

It became excellent training for my business future. One of my most treasured mentors, Marlene Lockard, chief of staff

> The people I met and partied with: Tipper Gore, Kevin Costner, Dr. Ruth Westheimer, Herbie Hancock, Billy Ray Cyrus–too many names to remember! It was fantastic. It happened because I was in love with taking action. I loved the adrenaline of taking action. I still do.

for Senator Bryan, taught me: "No permanent friends, no permanent enemies." You've got to be flexible in the situation. Wise counsel. Wise woman.

After a few years as press secretary to the attorney general, I had one more by-chance opportunity in politics. I was recruited for, and accepted a position as, deputy press secretary to Governor Miller, who had assumed the remainder of Richard Bryan's initial term and won twice on his own accord. Miller was constitutionally termed out as governor and had only a year left in office. I gladly served for his final year.

MOVING ON

I was offered a position in the newly elected successor governor's administration, but I ultimately declined as I had come to realize I wasn't really in love with politics. And so, my political career came to an end. I wasn't bummed out, though. I still believed in myself.

I spent the next five years working my way up from director of public relations to partner with a prestigious Nevada advertising agency. I had seemingly everything: the great salary, benefits, perks, prestige, expense account, car allowance, high-profile clients—the whole package. By then it had been quite a long time since thrift-store shopping for clothes, buying retreads for the car, or eating Top Ramen. The future looked bright. I was thankful to have "made it" to some degree.

After just five months loving my prestigious new position, my president asked me, "Where do you see yourself in five years?" Without hesitation I said, "I'll be a healer." Now, you're reading these words and thinking, "Well, that comes out of nowhere." It did for me too.

A SPIRITUAL JOURNEY

Nights, weekends, and holidays, for my personal pleasure, I collected and studied works from noted authors and speakers including Deepak Chopra, Michael Talbot, Andrew Weiss, Gary Zukav, Dr. Wayne Dyer, Louise Hay, W. Brugh Joy, Barbara Brennan, and many others. I listened to their tapes (cassettes) and read their books to myself and again out loud to Gary and our daughters. I was a metaphysicist at heart, interested in light, energy, spiritualism, human interaction, hypnosis, altered consciousness, the subconscious mind and paranormal activity of all kinds. Those interests were at the core of my being and ultimately represented in my social psychology bachelor's degree.

The president of my advertising agency said, "Have you ever been to a healer?" I hadn't. It was kind of awkward. She said she personally knew a healer whom she highly recommended to me. Fourteen days later I met Anya Lawrence, the director of the Healing Academy of Body, Mind and Light Science. One session with Anya and I was instantly at home. I traveled to the cosmos and back with new insight, natural ability, and extreme interest. I was invited to apply to her prestigious school and was at once accepted as an eager apprentice.

During my five-year program, I learned about the human/spiritual condition. Without getting too woo woo here, let me just say this: My education at The Academy equaled and exceeded everything I was taught in college. I am forever grateful to the universe, to Anya, to my guides and my colleagues, and mostly to Gary and my family who supported my absences and studies and willingly allowed me to work on them. I graduated with a certificate in Advanced Healing Techniques and Inter-Dimensional Awareness. I opened a healing studio and worked with paying clients for several years while also promoting and advancing in the ad agency and in the community.

I became a partner of the firm. I was at the pinnacle of a well-respected advertising and marketing institution and doing well at that. Still, it didn't resonate deeply with me. I was good at it. I excelled in it. I loved my partners, my president especially. I won awards, studied, and earned international accreditation in public relations, but ultimately I wasn't fulfilled. I didn't believe this was "it." I couldn't see the ad agency for the long haul.

Interestingly, Gary and I always talked about "if we could do anything together, anything at all, what would it be?" The answer never was simply, "We'd own a restaurant"; it was always, "We'd own the Squeeze In."

When the Squeeze In opportunity appeared out of nowhere, Gary and I leaped. And if it weren't for Gary, we might have never had the chance to begin with.

GARY DELIVERS THE BIG DREAM: SQUEEZE IN

Gary had steadily moved through the ranks of landscape construction for years, becoming a highly skilled big-tree specialist and a landscape foreman running jobs and crews, operating heavy equipment, and planting, moving, and removing giant specimen trees. He was a customer service magician, genuinely understanding the importance of excellent service and providing it. Among Gary's clients was Jerry Bussell, the owner of the Squeeze In.

Jerry was youthful, kind, and engaging. Knowing quality when he saw it, Jerry always requested Gary by name to plant trees at the gorgeous home he shared with his wife, Pat Lundvall. After each planting, Jerry always gave Gary his business card endorsed on the back with a gratuity, "Free breakfast for Gary's family," and that's how we were introduced to the Squeeze In. I imagine later, as he considered our business purchase price and the long-term building lease payments we poured back into his family, he recognized and appreciated the fantastic return on investment of those free breakfasts.

On our first trip we instantly fell in love with the place. And on each visit we'd say, "This place is so freaking cool."

There'd always been something truly remarkable about the Squeeze In's energy, long before we owned it. You feel the lovefest on entering, and we got that vibe *every single time we visited.*

At this point, though, even knowing his restaurant, I hadn't yet met Jerry Bussell. I had only admired his generosity and deeply appreciated his gratuities.

That was until a big political event in Reno, with Larry King as the featured speaker. My advertising agency bought a table at the event. Gary was with me as my agency partner gestured to a table over, fixing his tie and announcing to me, "We've got to go over there and say hello. That's Jerry Bussell, the governor's director of Homeland Security."

Even up to this point I had no idea this guy was the owner of the Squeeze In. My business colleague and I, dignified and respectful, made our way over to introduce ourselves and suddenly hubby Gary, came bounding in front of us, running up to the governor's representative. Gary excitedly called out, "Dude!" and threw his arms out. Bussell said, "Bro!" and threw his arms back. I stopped in my tracks, embarrassed, and astonished.

I'm thinking, "What's this craziness?" Gary whips around and says, "Misty, this is Jerry, owner of the Squeeze In." Stunned, I think, "Oh my gosh, how freaking cool is that!"

It was just awesome. And unexpected. Freakin' unexpected. And freakin' awesome.

OF RESTAURANTS AND SECURITY

Back at the ad agency, I got a call. Bussell was looking for a Homeland Security Department public information campaign, and he'd asked my agency to make a proposal. I developed the proposal, all the while thinking how cool it was that I was working on it for the owner of the Squeeze In, who just happened to be the director of Homeland Security. Yes, that was impressive. *But I was way more stoked about the Squeeze In credential.*

On the day of the meeting, Bussell arrived early, way before any of the partners. Still, it was no surprise to me Bussell was early. He was also a colonel in the U.S. Army National Guard. Those guys tend to be early, specific, and precise.

With plenty of time to talk, waiting for the others to arrive, we were simply chit-chatting about personal things, the weather, small talk. Among other things I said, "I'm so excited that you own the Squeeze In. You know, Gary and I, we both love the Squeeze."

Bussell said, "Yeah, it's such a great place." And then he gets down real low and all quiet. We're the only two people in the conference room. No one else would hear of course, because no one else was there.

"You know, I love the Squeeze In," he said. "I've had it for 26 years. I absolutely love it. It's a great business, but I'm—" and suddenly, he's down to a near whisper, "I'm thinking about selling it. I'm not putting it on the market or anything, but I'm thinking about selling it." As if on cue, the partners walked in.

I was dazed. I couldn't focus on anything about public information after that. But somehow I made it through the proposal and pitch, my heart racing for the Squeeze In. All I could think about and doodled on my notepad for the rest of the meeting was Squeeze In, Squeeze In, Squeeze In—oh yeah, Squeeze In.

Remember that part about Gary and me saying, "If we could do anything at all together, what would it be?"

At the end of the meeting we all shake hands and politely bid good day. Everybody's done. All the partners go back to their offices, and I sprint down the hall to my ad agency office, slam the door, and call Gary.

Leaping and jumping and out of breath, I say, "Gary, Gary, Gary. Oh my gosh, oh my gosh, you won't believe it. The Squeeze In's for sale." *We had literally dreamed and fantasized about this moment for years.*

We spent that night with minimal sleep, strategizing, dreaming, and talking. We kept repeating to each other, "We've got to get more information. We've got to figure it out. There's a reason this appeared in our lives at this time."

We knew that Jerry knew Gary from planting giant trees at his house, and Jerry knew me through politics and public relations, and he'd put it all together for the two of us. He clearly had this figured out, as if connecting the dots even before we were. Through the night, the clock ticked, tick, tick. I couldn't call him at 5:00 a.m. even though I was bright eyed. But hey, 7:00 a.m., colonel, U.S. Army National Guard—I knew this guy was up! I called his cell phone and I said, "Gary and I would like to talk with you about buying the Squeeze In." His excited words were, "You guys are the perfect couple for this." And so began the process.

After five months of numerous meetings, negotiation, business planning, a whole lot of creative financing, with prayers on top of it, contemplative stillness and a ton of action, Gary and I were the new owners of the Squeeze In.

I came in from that blizzard at the end of 2003, introduced by Jerry and Pat to a warm welcome from their former staff and a whole new kind of work. It was more than a physical journey. It was a metaphysical trek, a journey based on love and graciousness. The universe reached out and met us in trust, recognizing our desire, intent, and action. Together, Gary and I and our whole family had traveled the path from rags to restaurants, counting on each other and the universe throughout the entire journey.

"I couldn't wait for success, so I went ahead without it."
—JONATHAN WINTERS

In the 2006 movie *The Secret*, *Chicken Soup for the Soul* author Jack Canfield says we've all got our stories, many of sadness, fear, despair, and disappointment. He then says, "That's just 'So what?'" and goes on to say we become what we think about, what we take action on, who we *decide* to become. I've shared my rags story with you as an example of how being decisive and taking action brought change for me. I now hold the experience of my youth in high regard as where I am today is perfect in every way. I am thankful and happy and living my truth.

Full of energy and eager, Gary and I moved forward to fulfill our dreams. It wasn't always easy, and sometimes it was downright scary. Filled with appreciation for each other along with confidence in our love and energy, we pushed on. We hoped to ultimately find the means to be in control of our own time and to take our family to new heights.

CHAPTER THREE

Rocket Fuel for Restaurant Growth: The Main Ingredients

Have you ever been in love? With a person? An idea? Your restaurant?

Think about how great being in love feels. You're energetic, focused, alive, thrilled to be in the present moment, full of anticipation and excitement.

But then, somehow, unexpectedly, without a defined moment in time, some strange boredom might set in. You lose the glow. Things aren't as rosy. You get lazy. You don't act on your idea. You get mad at yourself. You fall out of love. The reality is you give up, defeated.

This is Defeat, with a big D. The problem with, and the beauty of, this kind of defeat is that it is self-inflicted. The good news is defeat can be conquered in one way and one way only: love yourself enough to take action!

If you use the process of falling in love, and strategically *apply the steps as a personal and business development tool*—this time in a focused, intentional manner—the results may shock, amaze, and thrill you.

> This is Defeat, with a big D. The problem with, and the beauty of, this kind of defeat is that it is self-inflicted. The good news is defeat can be conquered in one way and one way only: love yourself enough to take action!

If you could vastly improve your life just by deciding to, wouldn't you?

Love is about senses. We see, hear, taste, touch, and smell our way to love. Sometimes it's the way your love looks to you, sometimes the fragrance. Sometimes an idea pops into your head and it's the visual image of a great party that you love, a fabulous celebration, or grand opening, the visualization of when the idea has come to fruition. Sometimes you love hearing the imaginary applause. And sometimes you can even taste the celebratory champagne! Love is about sensation and feelings, *about emotion, the energy of motion. Energy + motion = emotion.* Feelings in action.

Falling in love is a beautiful thing. Thirty-four years ago, the 17-year-old me fell in love with 21-year-old Gary in just a couple days. Literally, the first time I saw him I was aflutter. It was a visual thing. He and his friends sauntered in to drop off a surfboard at a mutual friend's house and strutted back out the door with nary a word. Gary told me later, "I boogied my friends back down to their house, dropped them off, and said, 'I gotta jet back up there. There's a fox on the couch!'" (I know, it's so 70s!) Twenty minutes later, when Gary walked in the door, it clicked. Yes, just like that, it clicked. We both knew. We started giggling and smiling, our eyes locked in a gaze. We took action on our feelings.

Two weeks later we were engaged. Six months later we were married. After many years, our first daughter, Shila, was born and after thirteen years of marriage, our second daughter, Kay, came along. Yes, we got married for love, not pregnancy. I have been forever thankful that Gary and I both took action on the initial prompting, the attraction, the sensation! We sensed it. We knew. We put our energy in motion. We took action.

When I fell in love with the Squeeze In, it was similarly sensational: the smells of the fresh food got me, then the taste, the visual stimulation of it all. I loved it. I loved it for a dozen years before I figured out a way to buy it. And when I got to own it, I loved it enough to build sustainable systems. To work on it continuously and refine and create a living, breathing, supportive business that, at the time, employed just a dozen people. I'm so thankful for the love of my restaurant. Because I'm in love with it, I want to protect it as I do my marriage.

I was eager and excited and full of inspiration for each new day at the restaurant. Yes, I had my downtimes too. Of course I did; we all do. Days when I couldn't bring myself to even go into the restaurant and, days when I would devolve into exhaustion and angry outbursts (before Chad and Shila taught me many valuable people lessons!).

JUST DO IT!

What allowed my business to survive through the dark times, however, was the fact that I took action: relentlessly, tirelessly researching, designing, developing and implementing systems. I considered myself a "success hacker," always seeking the most direct route to effectiveness through systems. Then, the business could rely on the systems instead of my own spiritual and human energy. Thankfully, I figured out I could efficiently replicate my energy through systems. I loved my business. I was thankful for it, and I actively applied love and gratitude to sustain and grow it systematically with intention.

> What allowed my business to survive through the dark times, however, was the fact that I took action: relentlessly, tirelessly researching, designing, developing and implementing systems.

Injecting my spirit into systems had dual benefits: every action through a system carried my spiritual energy further, replicating the original love that went into systems design. Through refinement in the business, the systems got tighter, more efficient, and more easily adopted and replicated. The continuous development and refinement of systems were big keys to success, and it started with a spiritual concept: love.

I was in love with and thankful for my business and learned to give gratitude in every interaction.

The spiritual leader and author Joe Vitale says, "We must connect our brain and heart and gratitude to make great decisions. This is how and where to tap into the super/ subconscious mind. Our goal is to stay conscious in a state of gratitude." I endeavored to do this in the process of creating my systems at the Squeeze In.

I saw in my business a way to serve, to be kind, to give back. To paraphrase Michael Gerber in *The E-Myth Revisited*, the business exists for one purpose and that is to serve our personal goals, and our family goals. Part of my goal for the business is to provide a forum to serve others, to serve the universe.

FALL IN LOVE THROUGH GENEROSITY

I see owning a business as my chance to serve not only the needs of my family but of my community. I'm thankful for the chance to do it. Each year, my small restaurant chain is able to give generously to more than 300 charity groups and causes.

One strategy we've used successfully is to give beautifully wrapped, colorful, customized, gift baskets with gourmet coffee; full-color, Squeeze-logo coffee mugs; a menu; color sticker; and $25 gift certificate, useful for silent auctions, raffles, and other fundraising events. We wrap the whole thing up with festive cellophane and tissue paper, ribbons, and bows, and it makes a great presentation. We've heard for years, "You guys give to every cause!" Yes, we do.

You can give generously *and* do it on your terms. Our charity gift certificates have been "full value on weekdays" and "50% face value on holidays or weekends," when we're already slammed busy and don't want to give away the house on our big days. This way everyone wins.

Sometimes we don't even wait for groups to come to us. We see or hear about an event, and we call in, make contact, and find a way to be of service. We reach out, we offer. Why would we do this? Because we are thankful to have the means to be of service. Bob Proctor says, "What you appreciate appreciates!"

If you take a structured approach to falling back in love with your business, fuel your growth and development through gratitude, giving lovingly from your heart to your associates, guests, and your vendors and suppliers, you will be successful. Love and gratitude are like rocket fuel to your business AND your life!

YOU'RE SUPPOSED TO MAKE A PROFIT

The Go-Giver, by Bob Burg and John David Mann, is one of my all-time favorite business books. Whether training a new manager or professionally coaching a restaurant owner, this book is on their assignment list, and has been given as a personal gift from me to many. I highly encourage you to read it in full. It's a short, beautiful story, highlighted by the Five Laws of Stratospheric Success:

1. The law of value: your true worth is determined by how much more you give in value than you take in payment.
2. The law of compensation: your income is determined by how many people you serve and how well you serve them.
3. The law of influence: your influence is determined by how abundantly you place other people's interests first.
4. The law of authenticity: the most valuable gift you have to offer is yourself.
5. The law of receptivity: the key to effective giving is to stay open to receiving.

When falling in love, don't you do all these things almost automatically? What do you do to successfully woo a lover? You give, serve, influence, offer, and receive! You give energy, attention, eye contact, active listening, flowers, presents. It is the same process for falling back in love with your restaurant: You have to actively give feelings, energy, attention, look at it with new eyes, listen with new ears, and give it presents such as updated leadership, marketing, financial, operations, and product systems.

The Go-Giver is not a book about charity; it's an *insightful, strategic* business book. Your business is supposed to succeed, to earn a profit, make money. A fabulous goal for business owners is to fully engage each of the Five Laws of Stratospheric Success!

WHERE IS THE LOVE?

In the next chapter, I'll introduce you to the Five Irrefutable Laws of Restaurant Success, but for now, we've got a goal to fall in love—or back in love—with our businesses. On purpose. What we love, we protect and what we serve, we love.

> What we love, we protect and what we serve, we love.

Most independent restaurant owners say they started in this business *because they loved it.* They were so excited. Maybe you were just like that once upon a time.

You opened your restaurant. You loved it. Your guests loved it; they loved you.

Then you got into the daily grind. People got grumpy; you got grumpy. You got overwhelmed with all the behind-the-scenes business tasks, appearing more difficult than cooking or serving. And they stack up: accounts payables, scheduling, ordering, inventory, receiving procedures, financial and labor management, product consistency, catering contracts, service, hiring, training, tax returns, 941s. The list seems to go on forever.

You lost the excitement, the business end of it on top of the early mornings and late nights and working holidays and weekends. Taking care of yourself and your family wore you out. You end up frustrated just going into your restaurant. Is this sounding familiar? It's work now. It's not how you pictured it. But it can be, if you *fall back in love with your business,* through a planned, prioritized, strategic set of giving actions, founded in love and fueled on gratitude. Start with a gratitude list: Write down five things you're thankful for about your restaurant and five things you're thankful for in your life *because of your restaurant:*

1.
2.
3.
4.
5.
6.
7.
8.
9.
10.

As a reminder, Gary and I fueled our love for the Squeeze In with gratitude, at least a dozen years before we bought the place. *We loved it.* As we dreamed of the future, we'd say, "If we could do anything together, what would it be?" We never said, "We'd own a restaurant, or we'd buy a cafe." *We always said, "We'd own the Squeeze In."*

We very specifically called it out. "Gosh, wouldn't it be fun to own the Squeeze In? Wouldn't that be cool? Yeah, we'd dig it. It would be so much fun we'd love it."

We attracted the Squeeze to us through our love for it and then when we finally got there and actually owned it, we loved it and nurtured it. We loved and cared about our guests and served them with gratitude and kindness. We asked them their names. We made the extra effort to know and to serve them.

Here's a crazy story: When we bought the Squeeze, a seemingly grouchy old guy came in all the time, a very regular guest over the years.

This guy would grunt out his order without eye contact and never smile. One day I asked a server who had been with the Squeeze for nearly two decades, "What's the guy's name on table 5? He never smiles." She replied, "I don't know his name." I was appalled.

I said, "You've been here for seventeen years, and you don't know his name?"

"Grumpy? I have his order memorized." She had a crazy laugh. "But no, I don't know his real name."

"Don't you think that might be an important thing?" I asked her. This guy was at the Squeeze more than weekly. Well guess what? That very morning, I sat down with him and learned his and his wife's names.

Of course, he started coming in even more often, bringing his wife most times. Guess what else? He smiled every time he came in and made eye contact. He was no longer some grumpy, grouchy, old guy eating breakfast. He had become a happy guest because someone *cared enough to ask his name while sharing genuine attention and kindness.*

You probably already know this important concept, but do your associates? Do you have a system in place to assure they're working to learn your guest's names and preferences? Are guests greeted warmly and genuinely by name, whenever possible? What are your service standards? Are they articulated in a system? Do your associates know *exactly* what you want them to say, and when and how to say it? If not, why not?

> He had become a happy guest because someone *cared enough to ask his name while sharing genuine attention and kindness.*

And that's one tiny little thing. What else can you do? Can you have the front and back of the house know each other's names? They don't have to fall in love with each other, but could they have common courtesy and kindness for each other? Could the servers know the dishwashers' names? Could they say to each other once in a while, "How can I help you? What can I do to be of service to you?" What is all that based on? *It's all based on love. And it all starts with YOU.* Give energy and kindness to receive it in all areas of your life, including in your restaurant.

SERVING EACH OTHER: KINDNESS AND COURTESY CAN MAKE A COMEBACK!

My background mantra is "Thank You," on each heartbeat. All the time. Each time my heart beats, thank you, *thank you*. And, how may I serve? These thoughts are written around my office, on my phone, on little stickers at my desk and home—everywhere I turn. "Thank you. How may I serve you?"

My friend Tim Paulson, author of the book *Love and Grow Rich: How to Love Your Way to Life's Riches,* said, "We love those whom we serve. If you want to love someone to a greater degree, do something to serve them."

Isn't serving others the basis of love? Doesn't that mean—by extension—just being in the restaurant business is an extension of love? I think so. I think if we can come at this from a foundation of love, love first for God, for the universe, for ourselves, our families, our communities, love for and falling back in love with our business, love energy comes and supports us when we stay open to receive it. We can't do anything without energy and the foundation of all energy is love.

> Isn't serving others the basis of love? Doesn't that mean–by extension–just being in the restaurant business is an extension of love?

Paulson also said, "Love is a special word. Use it freely and often. The more you say it, the more you'll feel it—and the richer in love you will grow!"

The truly secret recipe is to love your associates, your guests, and your business, and take action on your love. Love for what you do as well as love for yourself and your family and all that you have. Love is fueled by gratitude. Be thankful, appreciative for everything in your life. Seek all the positives and focus on them. Love is like soft, cushiony flour and action is the yeast that makes it rise.

Deepak Chopra suggests we find success in life when we start by loving what we already have. What a great perspective! Instead of lusting after what you want, how 'bout loving what you have?

Dr. Joe Vitale says, "Gratitude attracts more things to be grateful for."

Here's how I know my partners and I have been successful in creating a culture of love and gratitude in our business. In autumn 2012, a local TV station did a piece on the Squeeze because we had just been featured in the *New York Times* (remember that whole thing earlier about being ready? We were ready!). The TV station knew about this because the local newspaper, the *Reno Gazette Journal,* had recapped the *New York Times* piece. Upon seeing that, the TV station wanted to come by. Media coverage often inspires more media coverage and attention in turn.

Now, when the cameras arrived at the Squeeze, no one had prepped my niece, General Manager Amanda Martinez, on what to say. She had no talking points, no message sheet;

it was completely spontaneous. With camera and a microphone, the reporter asked Amanda, "Why do you think this place is successful?" With a big smile, Amanda looked into the camera and said, "Because we love our guests. When you love your guests, they keep coming back." That's exactly how it happened!

No one coached her. No one told her what to say. Amanda is immersed in a culture, a company that cares. It's a culture she's helped create and inspires daily as one of our longest serving associates. In fact, even in our company mission statement, we say we're in business to serve our guests, *our associates, and communities.* It's not only about making money. It's not only about being profitable and successful. We're in business to serve our guests, our associates, and our communities while earning a living for our families. We encourage our associates to serve each other in the same way that we serve them. We think it's important to be loving, kind, and courteous.

"Acknowledging the good that you already have in your life is the foundation for all abundance." That's from Eckhart Tolle's *A New Earth: Awakening to Your Life's Purpose.*

LOVERS AND HATERS

The world is full of love and it pays to stay focused on it. It's also true there's anger and hatred out there. What you think about expands, becomes your reality. Thoughts literally have a gravitational force, bringing more of what you focus on into your daily life, into the moment. Love creates its own support structure while hatred divides and weakens individuals, families, systems, and businesses—in fact, whole societies. Carefully protect your thoughts and keep the negativity at bay. Your job is to build a fortress around your mind. Negativity is the ultimate enemy. *You must actively defend against it at all cost.* Willie Nelson says, "Once you replace negative thoughts with positive ones, you'll start having positive results."

The Internet creates opportunities for haters to show up in the form of e-bullies. People often hide behind mostly anonymous or fictitious review profiles to unjustly trash your business. Recent media stories highlight businesses paying their staff to write negative reviews of competitors. Sometimes disgruntled former employees do the deed. While you do have to monitor and respond, you don't have to stay focused on the negativity.

Be mindful of the parable about the angry man who grabs a piece of burning coal to hurl at his enemy. He gets burned before he can even throw it.

Negativity cloaked in anonymity is part of the Internet territory. If you focus on the hate and anger, it will take you down. You must allow that negative vibration to live outside your mindset. Let that energy remain with the people who create it. Insulate yourself from it. Focus instead on your love for your restaurant, your guests, associates, for your family, for God, or the universe, however you say it, and for your community: your friends and neighbors. *Start making everything you do based on love.* The love vibration will run throughout your body and business and *love is attractive.* Be gracious, full of gratitude. *Gratitude is attractive.* Love and gratitude attract success. *Success is attractive.* See the cycle?

Focusing on negativity, the hate of the world, the ugly things on the news, and the yuckiness out there is like sending angry arrows out from your energetic field to repel people, repel business. Love and gratitude attracts; negativity repels. If you have TVs in your business, *try turning off the news!* You might find positive programming makes for a better mood and feeling in your restaurant. Personally, I can't stand supporting businesses where murders, robberies, and disasters are playing out on screens in every direction.

During my studies at the Healing Academy, I learned to create energy structures or thought templates to develop new ideas, learning, or actual things. Like many folks, I also use vision boards to help solidify an intention, to help show a completed project, to keep it front and center on my "mental screen." There's power in imagery, visualization, meditation, and contemplation. I spend time regularly to boost my love energy using these techniques.

> There's power in imagery, visualization, meditation, and contemplation.

FALLING IN LOVE

I have created a thought-based energetic template, a foundation of love in myself, my family, in our business to arrive at this position today. The fact that we own four successful and growing restaurants—busy restaurants that are getting all kinds of attention—is a result of that energetic hacking. It started in my mind as thought. Then, sharing the vision, together, Gary, Shila, Chad, and I added love (emotion) and gratitude to get here.

Deepak Chopra said, "Humans have an average of 65,000 thoughts each day. The problem is that 95 percent of them are the same thoughts as the day before!" Think something new! Remember, our goal is to fall back in love with our restaurants and fuel our love with gratitude.

We've all heard if we "do what we love, the money will follow," but Paulson, in *Love and Grow Rich,* suggests instead, "When you LOVE WHAT YOU ARE DOING, regardless of what it is, you will be more successful at it … whether you are self-employed or work for someone else … when you love what you do, it makes a world of difference." Start loving what you're doing now! Start with questions: What do I most love about my restaurant? What do I love about my associates? What do I love about my guests?

FIVE STEPS TO FALL IN LOVE:

Step 1: Focus on love; feel good.

Step 2: Add your physical senses; visualize!

Step 3: Fuel with gratitude; what are you thankful for?

Step 4: Create a plan; write your steps down; ask and answer questions.

Step 5: Take action!

Ongoing: Measure your results and begin the feedback loop over again after making any necessary adjustments.

Will Rogers understood the value of feedback. He said, "Even if you're on the right track, you'll get run over if you just sit there." Keep feeding in information and taking action!

This book, *From Rags to Restaurants* is also part of my love-based energy "thought" template. Before writing it, I created an energetic structure in spirit and thought—an energetic template. I have since filled the template with chapters and words. We've been featured by the *New York Times, Wall Street Journal,* the *Reno Gazette Journal, Powder* magazine, *National Geographic World,* the *San Francisco Chronicle,* and many more as well as on TV and radio and all over the Internet. This came because I began visualizing it, long ago, working on my business, not in my business. I started first by thinking of it and then seeing what I wanted to create. Seeing it physically and in my visual field, on my "mental screen," the mind's eye, or, simply, visualization.

Napoleon Hill, in *Think and Grow Rich*, quoted poet Ella Wheeler Wilcox:

> *You never can tell what a thought will do*
> *In bringing you hate or love—*
> *For thoughts are things, and their airy wings*
> *Are swifter than carrier doves.*
> *They follow the law of the universe—*
> *Each thing creates its kind,*
> *And they speed o'er the track to bring you back*
> *Whatever went out from your mind.*

I disagree with the first line *because we know exactly what our thoughts will do.* Just look around at what you've created in your life and business and you can see actual former thoughts in reality. Our thoughts are incredibly powerful things operating at the speed of light with energy and frequency. We must guard carefully what we put in our minds and what we allow to come out, staying true to what we want. *Know too what you don't want but know it for contrast only; don't dwell on it. One thought—for contrast. One and done.*

In *Think and Grow Rich,* Hill says, "Love is, without question, life's greatest experience. It brings one into communion with Infinite Intelligence." I'd even take it one step further, by saying: love is the language of success in all things and *gratitude and appreciation is love's currency.*

Does it sound crazy to be in love with your business? Some may find it a little too West Coast, a little too hippie.

Yet, if you could connect with Infinite Intelligence for the success of your business, wouldn't that be a valuable activity to pursue? Especially since it's 100 percent free.

As an independent restaurateur, I've discovered I'm in the public relations business and the systems design and development business. I'm in analytics and metrics. I'm in leadership, marketing, operations, and financial management. Oh, *and* I'm in the food and entertainment business. Remember that "cute little café" dream? What?

I believe love coupled with action is the quintessential secret recipe in business success. I think it's the rocket fuel, the turbo charger!

Love, like every daily action we take as independent restaurateurs, adds up. Over time, it multiplies and, just like money in a savings account, it compounds. We've got to protect our precious time and thoughts, staying focused and active on what is meaningful to us, what matters to us, what helps us meet our goals and live our dreams. We have to be intentional in our daily approach.

I believe love coupled with action is the quintessential secret recipe in business success. I think it's the rocket fuel, the turbo charger!

INGREDIENTS FOR SUCCESS

1. Write a gratitude list every day.
2. Create a system to learn and use guest names.
3. Use the word love ten times today and every day. Make it a part of your regular vocabulary
4. Acknowledge the good you already have in your life; it's attractive!
5. Avoid negativity at all cost.
6. Intentionally take the Five Steps to Fall in Love.

CHAPTER FOUR

The Five Irrefutable Laws of Restaurant Success

That first month at the Squeeze In, I took only a half-day off. It was day 17 when I went skiing. For nearly three solid weeks, by day, I served guests and learned the recipes, how we prepped our products, and special omelette techniques, and I bused tables. At night I worked on lists, ideas, and the beginning of systems development. I had already let the bookkeeper go, so I was also learning how to use Quick-Books, pay vendors, process payroll, state sales tax returns, and more. It was a lot of detail, but we all know the devil is in the details. So is the money.

While the Squeeze would turn 30 years old just four months after we bought it, as far as I was concerned, it was essentially a brand-new business. It worked really well in many areas. It had great flow and was efficient, but I knew it had to be dialed down, honed in, and tuned up. It had to be if we were to continue to serve the many loyal patrons, earn a living for our family, pay vendors, make payroll, and give generously to our community.

I constantly strove to further develop and maintain the easy-going, hippie, loving, laid-back restaurant ambiance up front, while working nonstop to become as sophisticated and efficient as IBM behind the scenes.

> I constantly strove to further develop and maintain the easy-going, hippie, loving, laid-back restaurant ambiance up front, while working nonstop to become as sophisticated and efficient as IBM behind the scenes.

I started with *not one thing but many things.* As Dan Kennedy says, "Little hinges swing big doors." I gathered notes during my days working the floor and wrote lists at night, the separate parts beginning to come together to form systems. It wasn't just theoretical; it was functional; it was real.

I studied and compared our supply delivery invoices and took them in person to Sam's Club and Costco and built spreadsheets to ease price comparisons. Because Sam's Club did "fax and pull," making business service that much more efficient by having our order on pallets with a single invoice, and because I was able to demonstrate an immediate annual savings of $25,000 by hand shopping, I asked Gary to quit his landscape construction job. While the savings wasn't even close to his salary, I knew we could make it, and I relished the extra time with my best friend.

Just three months into Squeeze ownership, Gary gave his notice at the landscaping firm and has never looked back (ironically, nearly 10 years later, he still regularly has landscape dreams in his sleep!). Gary became our shopping, errand, and maintenance guy and on weekends was the most amazing busboy and Bloody Mary seller while giving superior guest service. He truly embodied what we would later come to call the WOW guest experience.

Gary's new full-time commitment to the Squeeze allowed me to concentrate on developing my leadership skills: the ability to see the big picture; plan for success; create better rapport with our associates and guests; and identify training opportunities. I was able to influence Squeeze employees, lead them in new ways of delivering excellent guest service while tuning up operational efficiency. Many of them saw the advantages and new levels of security *and opportunity* in their positions. Those who couldn't handle change either self-selected and moved on or were promoted to guest.

ASKING QUESTIONS

For me, each day ended with the personal question "What could I have done to be more effective today?" and the business question "What could we have done better today to serve our guests and the business?" I knew early on the importance and value of asking questions and did so continuously. I've found one important component of leadership is the constant focus on refining, improving. Just because something works doesn't mean it can't be fine-tuned. I often say *if we're not refining, we're declining.* Decline is not an ideal leadership state.

I'm a questioner, finding many ways to get to the answers. I question everything in a constant search of truth in all areas of life. Some of my personal truths are these: faith, family, fitness and finances, in that order. While at the Healing Academy, I studied in depth the chakra system and the qualities associated with each of these seven main energy metabolizers. From the base, physical, and moving up, emotional, mental, social (love), will, spirit. I strive always for balance, harmony and health in the complex interplay between the energy body (template) and the physical body, between structure and flow.

In seeking health in all areas, if I'm not standing in my truth, I'm in discordance, disharmony. My goal in life is to create health in all aspects of my being and in my businesses and to assist my clients in doing so. Sick businesses can't be of service to the owners, their families, associates, or community. Sick owners can't be of service either. Focusing on and developing health allows me to give more, serve more, and add more value to others. Creating harmony and balance in life requires that we make a decision to move forward, keep our thoughts in accordance with our decision, and, most importantly, take action. It's not complex; it just takes discipline and commitment. I never want to stop learning.

THE FIVE IRREFUTABLE LAWS OF RESTAURANT SUCCESS

No restaurant can enjoy long-term success without carefully upholding the Five Irrefutable Laws of Restaurant Success. Thanks to years of study and growth, I've been able to hack into this success code and am eager to share it with you. My dominant goal in *From Rags to Restaurants,* is to be of service to you, to help and add value to your restaurant, family, associates, guests and community. I love people. I love this industry, and I love to serve, so it is with great joy I serve as your personal restaurant success hacker. Get ready for a big download of information!

To set the stage for the Five Irrefutable Laws, we must first have context. Our context is strategy, tactics, accountability, results, or STAR.

Every action we take in the day-to-day management of our restaurants must be strategic—in other words, *part of the plan.* Strategy is your plan, plain and simple. Decide what you want to accomplish and write it down. Tactics are simply the activities you will take to achieve your strategy to complete your plan. Accountability is your promise to yourself. Keep it. Results—and this is the crucial factor—is what you review and feed back (or drop if the result is unsatisfactory) into this powerful closed-loop system for continuous improvement. Each time results are fed back into the strategy, the STAR context becomes stronger, more focused and better executed—in other words, more successful.

Within the STAR context, we can now discuss the Five Irrefutable Laws of Restaurant Success: leadership, operations, financials, products/services, and marketing.

THE FIVE IRREFUTABLE LAWS OF RESTAURANT SUCCESS

1. The law of leadership: the ability to influence. Our job as business leaders is to model personal growth and expect successful behavior while we develop and hold ourselves and our associates accountable.

2. The law of operations: every aspect of the business is systematized to efficiently and effectively meet stated goals through planning, policies, procedures, and measured performance.

THE FIVE IRREFUTABLE LAWS OF RESTAURANT SUCCESS

3. The law of financials: with integrity and diligence, financials and products are tracked, monitored, and adjusted to assure financial health, fitness, and profitability.

4. The law of products/services: our products must be reliable and we must diligently serve our customers and associates with courtesy, appreciation, respect, and kindness.

5. The law of marketing: the business must use multimedia tools to communicate in a timely manner with guests and associates in relevant, meaningful ways.

In the restaurant, guests and associates are the centerpiece of the Five Irrefutable Laws of Restaurant Success and live at the focal point, the intersection of the law of leadership, the law of products/services, and the law of marketing. The foundation of the Five Irrefutable Laws of Restaurant Success are the law of operations and the law of financials. No business of any kind stands long without strength in those two critical footings.

Successful restaurateurs will see themselves and their restaurants reflected in the image below. Those seeking true restaurant success will find it through building core competencies in each of the Five Irrefutable Laws of Restaurant Success.

The great news is we'll discuss each of the five laws in subsequent chapters, and we'll start with a discussion on leadership.

Law #1, the law of leadership, at the top of our STAR is the high point of success in the restaurant business.

As I've already said, I love learning and I'm not done yet. I'm truly addicted. I'll never stop! I'm thrilled to be a certified member of the John Maxwell Team, having studied coaching, speaking and training. I study with Maxwell's professional faculty as well as directly with John Maxwell, one of the most recognized and celebrated leadership voices in the world. I'm thrilled for the fantastic opportunity to share John

Maxwell's wisdom. As is widely known, when the student is ready, the teacher appears.

Maxwell says, "Not everyone will become a great leader, *but everyone can become a better leader.*" I'm not a great leader, but I'm a great student and listener, always eager to learn and grow. I put personal growth and development on my agenda every day. My brilliant husband, Gary Young, says, "If it's not on your list, it doesn't exist." Well said.

"Leadership is influence, nothing more and nothing less," John Maxwell says. Maxwell's approach proves leaders don't develop in a day but *through daily development.* In my effort to develop the Squeeze and myself, I hit it hard, working, studying, and growing on a daily basis. *The daily agenda matters.*

FOCUSING ON SYSTEMS

As the new owner of the Squeeze, I asked many questions and I listened. I took massive notes, wrote lists and ideas and drafted an operations manual focused on "processes, systems, and efficiencies." It became the early backbone of our systems development, the Bible for everything we did on a daily basis. The operations manual contained opening and closing checklists, vendor and maintenance phone numbers, scripts, purchase and delivery schedules, inventory processes and more. I still have the original printed manual from nearly a decade ago. Those faded, yellowing pages have cheese sauce, coffee stains, Post-it notes and lots of handwritten scribbles all over them. My goal was to leave no question unanswered.

The operations manual was a monumental task but well worth it. We could never have quadrupled our business from one location to four without it, and many subsequent iterations and additional systems have evolved from that initial effort. More importantly, we never would have survived the first year alone without taking on such a labor and mentally intensive process.

Working daily in the restaurant, serving guests, taking orders, pouring coffee, cooking omelettes, sweeping floors, closing out the drawer, attending merchant association meetings and chamber events, and then writing, doing systems development, marketing, payroll, inventory, and burning the midnight oil took its toll on me. I knew what most leaders come to realize: You ultimately have to work to your strengths. I was a good server. I wasn't excellent, I didn't love it. Cooking? Love it, but not on the commercial cooking line. Attending community meetings? I had to find new ways to be effective with my time.

> I knew what most leaders come to realize: You ultimately have to work to your strengths.

On change, Maxwell says, "Change is inevitable. Growth is optional," and he trains his team members to play to their strengths. My strengths? I'm a visionary, can get to the 30,000-foot view very fast, with precision. Love strategy (planning), marketing, and communications. Love being in the media, on TV, in the newspaper, in the spotlight. Love designing systems, teaching others how to make them work flawlessly and tinkering and adjusting when they don't. Love the challenge of creation. Don't like doing the day-to-day part. Love being an idea generator. Love people. Not big on the daily grind. Love the big picture. The details? Not so much. I was intentional about playing to my strengths and seeking to surround myself with people who could support me in the details.

The world's number-one small business guru Michael E. Gerber, author of *The E-Myth Revisited: Why Most Small Businesses Don't Work and What to Do About It*, addresses the critical nature of working on your business: "Indeed, the problem is not that the owners of small businesses in this country don't work; the problem is that *they're doing the wrong work.* As a result, most of their businesses end up in chaos, unmanageable, unpredictable, and unrewarding." I didn't want that for me, my family, or the Squeeze and its families.

Once I realized I could best serve my company, my family, my associates, and guests by completely transforming my role, I elevated to leadership exclusively, living law #1, the law of leadership, to the benefit of all of us. I went to that place of working only on the business, not in it. I applaud my business partners Gary, Shila, and Chad. Without their encouragement and support of my leadership and continued development, we may not have been able to fully explore new opportunities and offers.

FAILING FORWARD

A restaurant with a lengthy history and good reputation just a few doors from the Squeeze quietly became available for sale and we were approached as potential buyers. We were excited as this deal would have given us the opportunity to be in both the breakfast/lunch *and* the lunch/dinner/bar business. It had a full liquor license (at the time we had only a beer/wine license) and tons of potential. We could see the possibility of cross-promoting the two businesses and, having just spent two years developing incredibly detailed systems, we felt truly prepared.

For us, the big-ticket item we sought was to purchase the business, and ultimately the building. It had long been our goal to own commercial real estate. However, after substantial effort, legal counsel, accounting advice, financial investment, business planning, development of the corporate entity, transfer of the liquor license, and announcements to and meetings with the restaurant's existing staff as well as the Squeeze staff, the deal fell apart at the eleventh hour. We left the failed bid with a sizable cash loss, bruised reputation and feelings, and—ultimately—an understanding that *the universe had protected us in the biggest way.* As always, we learned many important lessons from the failure and moved forward.

Remembering the lesson to work to our strengths, we returned focus to the Squeeze with renewed vision, purpose, and energy. We modernized and expanded our menu with the addition of burgers and fries—we had long lamented guests' incredulous question, *"You don't serve burgers and fries?"* as they then headed several doors down to the other place. We knew if we were going to get bigger, better, faster, more profitable, we had to also expand our thinking and our approach. Our little restaurant was closed more hours of the day than it was open. We decided to open for dinner at the Squeeze. It didn't turn out to be a strength.

While the overall dinnertime math was good, the numbers were inconsistent. One night we'd serve well over a hundred guests and the next night we'd serve 16. Guests raved about our home-cooked products and great service, but the whole family and our associates were completely exhausted. We did dinner for almost six months before pulling the plug. Another defeat. I was convinced, however, that this brand, this company, this family would extend. I was right.

One important lesson of leadership is to know when you need help, *and to seek it.* It's often said we are the sum total of the five people we most associate with.

Maxwell says, "Teams make you better than you are, multiply your value, enable you to do what you do best, allow you to help others do their best, give you more time, provide you with companionship, help you fulfill the desires of your heart and compound your vision and effort." I decided it would be smart to find more associates better aligned with my business goals.

I gracefully bowed out of the many boards and committees I had been associating with. The grandstanding, infighting, the long, unfocused meetings, and general lack of vision had been energetically draining. I began to seek out restaurant-specific leaders and mentors, people whose skills would immediately benefit me and the Squeeze. I joined a restaurant industry mastermind group and started studying every book and resource I could get my hands on. After two years of Squeeze ownership, I took a deep breath and kind of started over. Again.

The first year we owned the Squeeze, gross revenues increased 20 percent over the prior year, and through systematization, we drove expenses down. Annually since, we've grown revenues or added a location. Now with four locations, our annual revenues are nearly eight times what they were on day one. Each time we've expanded the company, we've poured ourselves and our personal resources right back in. We've taken some hard hits in the process and haven't been unscathed.

In his book, *No B.S. Business Success,* Dan Kennedy's Eternal Truth #3 is: "Failure is part of the daily entrepreneurial experience." Kennedy's Eternal Truth #4 is: "How you deal with failure determines whether or not you ever get the opportunity to deal with success."

The following story is difficult to tell: *we hit the bottom with a thud.*

RENO OR BUST: SQUEEZE IN #2

With the failed restaurant purchase and subsequent dinner experiment behind us, we began to explore sophisticated marketing systems and the idea of a second location. We errantly believed the majority of our guests were coming from "over the hill," which meant the Sacramento area, not "down the hill," which, folks in Truckee know, means Reno. By analyzing our newly launched birthday club membership, we were shocked to find almost 65 percent were from the Reno area, just 30 miles away and where Gary and I had lived the previous 25 years. Shila and Chad lived in Reno too and that sealed the deal. We set our sights on Reno and started planning.

In early 2007, just months after the failed restaurant purchase bid and failed dinner experiment, we found a great location, wrote a comprehensive business plan, negotiated and signed a long-term lease, and wrote big checks for deposits. It seemed that as fast as the construction moved forward, the economy moved backward and tightened. Every businessperson knows where the economy began in 2007 and where it went from there. Every loan possibility dried up. Every bank said no. The Small Business Administration (SBA) said no. Every yes quickly became an unreturned phone call. Every friend, family member, and potential business lender who had said yes, or maybe yes, started back-peddling.

We had already maxed out every single resource we personally owned. Every shred of credit had been leveraged, every favor called in, every place to shave costs had been shaven. The Reno construction train was too far down the path to stop the motion; it simply had to go forward. The second restaurant had to open or we risked losing everything. If the cash flow didn't start, we'd go bankrupt, and that wasn't an option for us, our families, or our associates.

The hardest conversation I'd had in years was with the construction company building out the restaurant. I said, "The money's gone. We're supposed to open in a few weeks. We're busted and on the very edge." They replied with the best eight words I'd heard in a very long time:

We love your vision.
We believe in you.

Yeah, I bolded, underlined and italicized that. It was huge for us, for me personally.

The contract was rewritten, and the build-out was mortgaged through our lease. We opened our second location February 1, 2008, with 100 percent of first-day gross sales donated to charity. The cash did start flowing, but even so, we still weren't able to overcome the ever-mounting debt burden, and we continued to dive upside down as the country began to spiral faster into the

We were simultaneously thrilled with guests pouring in the door and terrified the debt load would crush us.

depths of the Great Recession. We were simultaneously thrilled with guests pouring in the door and terrified the debt load would crush us.

I began to renegotiate every debt we had. We didn't stiff any of our creditors or walk away from any of our accounts. Instead, in full honesty and forthrightness, I personally negotiated in a courteous, straightforward, and businesslike manner. I took the continuous stream of nasty phone calls and was polite to every person regardless of his/her demeanor. I talked with lenders, collection agencies, lawyers. I sent and received letters, e-mails, and faxes while keeping meticulous notes in up-to-date file folders and spreadsheets. Strategic negotiation absolutely saved us from bankruptcy and after just a few years, our business credit has recovered and we currently carry zero lines of credit. I've learned many difficult and humbling lessons in this school.

On failure, mentor Maxwell says, "'Failing forward' is the ability to get back up after you've been knocked down, learn from your mistake, and move forward in a better direction." And, lest we think the path easy for anyone, American inventor Thomas Edison said, "I haven't failed. I've found 10,000 ways that don't work."

We've been moving forward ever since, making it our goal to learn, adapt, and keep growing. Some of the most amazing things I've learned have come from my partners. Shila, while young, is ever wise, models extreme patience and attentive, reflective listening. Shila is the peacemaker in our partnership. Gary has taught me so much about getting things done. He has more energy than most and gets more done before noon than many people do in a couple days. Chad has been the champion of the employees, and I credit him for helping me make a fundamental shift in approach from where I began with "processes, systems, efficiency" to "*people*, systems, efficiency."

CREATING A SUCCESSFUL TRIBE

From the outset, I saw the entire employee contingent of the Squeeze In as a business transaction, saying often, "They sell labor and we buy it. If they don't like the way we do it, they can sell their labor to someone else." I was adamant in my hard-nosed approach that "this is business." I was impatient and demanding, all the while believing myself to be compassionate.

Even during those early years of Squeeze ownership, I was finishing my advanced certification from the Healing Academy of Body, Mind and Light Science, intensely studying inner peace, prayer, kindness, compassion, patience, and love. At the same time, I compartmentalized and segregated two sides of my being: the loving, kind, easy, content, interested person, with the hard-driving, by-the-book, numbers and statistics fanatic who could be unpredictable and quick to anger. Unfortunately, I saw employees as a business problem, not part of the solution. Through his leadership, Chad shed light on the true importance of our employees, on the partnership aspect. He told me that happy employees made for happy guests. They were there for more than just a paycheck. They didn't just "sell labor"; *they gave life energy to the business, which helped it shine brightly.* They wanted to be loved and would love in return.

Once I "got it," everything shifted. Again.

As our leader, I began in earnest to develop comprehensive multimedia training programs, starting where I was most familiar, the front of the house. I now more deeply understood the dynamics and critical nature of the only two types of people in the restaurant: guests *and associates.* Even our language changed. "Employees" were gone; "associates" were here to stay. My personal approach changed. I had exclusively focused on the guest in the past. I realized how much more balanced the company would be, how much more genuine it would be if we loved our associates as much as we loved our guests.

I've studied many great leadership teachers, but more importantly, have put their ideas to use in my business and in my life. I have a long way to go. I still make a lot of mistakes and put my foot in my mouth too often, but I forgive myself and keep trudging on, reading, learning,

> Happy employees made for happy guests. They were there for more than just a paycheck. They didn't just "sell labor"; they gave life energy to the business, which helped it shine brightly. They wanted to be loved and would love in return.

growing, implementing, and still occasionally washing my footprints out of my mouth.

Leadership guru Ken Blanchard teamed up with Garry Ridge in the book *Helping People Win at Work,* which has added immensely to my leadership knowledge and to the Squeeze's overall approach to our associates, our training, and the value we offer our guests and the communities we serve. The essential message of this great book is summed up by these words: "When you lead at a higher level, the development of the people you're leading is just as important as the performance and results you desire."

Yep.

The idea of leading in a partnership of mutual trust and respect, creating a two-way influence stream with benefit to all participants was really new thinking to me. We approached the development of our training program as a way to help our associates be happy at work. Ridge told a story of how, when he was a professor, he was chastised for handing out to his college students the final exam on the first day of class. He responded to the criticism by saying, "Not only will I give them the final exam ahead of time, what do you think I'll do throughout the semester? *I'll teach them the answers so that when they get to the final exam, they'll get As.* You see, I think life is all about helping people get As, not forcing them into a normal distribution curve."

Ridge's quote floored me and propelled me into reading the rest of the book fast. It was one of those "hacker" moments when I realized I had found some truly deep and meaningful wisdom. I let it facilitate the further development and refinement of our comprehensive training and performance evaluation systems.

What our team has done well as leaders—our entire partnership team, myself, Gary, Shila, and Chad, as well as our Squeeze management team, has been to use experts, ideas, and systems, with proven ways to cut down on the learning curve, reducing the time it takes to get from A to B. This fast-track approach means we're not recreating the wheel. We've successfully used this method to develop our completely customized training program with manuals, checklists, live-in-person training, a series of nine videos, and accompanying quiz. After our original set of videos, a newly revised version has been produced by President Shila, all available via my website, www.mistyyoung.com.

We've hacked a fast-track learning method, seeking the right experts with the right information to develop our Superstar Hiring Profile, and to gain additional expertise in recipe costing, cost control systems, and financial management. We've made it our business to learn *and keep learning*— the law of leadership in action!

With the knowledge gained from *Helping People Win at Work,* we created the Squeeze In Code of Business Conduct and refined our associate approach to be more tribe-like. Ridge says, "A tribe is a place you belong; a team is something you play on once in a while." While a code of business conduct might seem to be overkill for a mom-and-pop (and Gaga-and-Papa, thanks to Shila and Chad's twins, Emerie and Wesley) restaurant company, we knew it was smart to emulate the best of the best, *so we did.*

We worked on our company culture, a culture of service not only to the guest, but associate to associate. We modeled the Squeeze's Partnering for Performance associate evaluation program straight from the materials in the book. With this innovative process, associates evaluate themselves in a presentation to their managers for discussion and development. Managers prepare their own evaluations and present to regional managers and regional managers present to owners. This approach has been tremendously successful.

Our job descriptions became much clearer, more understandable, standards and accountability built right in. A central tenet of the *Helping People Win at Work* strategy is accountability through clear expectations. Your associates aren't mind readers. Having developed clear goals for each position in the restaurant, our managers were better able to help their associates get As on their final exam (performance evaluation). This approach also meant we could measure and mentor managers if their folks weren't getting As because the system is designed to support success. Even after going through our sophisticated live audition, hiring, training, and development process, not everyone makes it through the rigorous, 90-day, probationary period. (We still love them, though.)

While leadership development has been and continues to be a daily process filled with successes and sometimes hard lessons, I wouldn't change it. I believe leadership development and continued personal growth are the promises of true human potential. I wish leadership were taught in elementary school.

Keep in mind the simple truth of the law of leadership: the ability to influence. Our job as business leaders is to model personal growth and expect successful behavior while we develop and hold ourselves, and our associates, accountable.

We've already seen how the second law, the law of operations, is about systematizing. The law states: every aspect of the business is systematized to efficiently and effectively meet stated goals through planning, policies, procedures, and measured performance.

The five laws build on and strengthen each other for a well-balanced, profitable, successful restaurant. We'll examine each of them in turn.

INGREDIENTS FOR SUCCESS

1. Be accountable to using a structured calendar daily.
2. Start asking more questions. Start now. Just asking, "What questions should I ask?" will begin to bring new answers.
3. Make STAR part of every day. Be strategic, tactical, accountable, and results oriented.
4. Post the Five Irrefutable Laws of Restaurant Success above your desk (printable version at website).
5. As systems ideas pop into your head, put them on your calendar immediately.

6. Post "If it's not on your list, it doesn't exist" where you can read it daily.

7. Gracefully bow out of time-sucking or non mission-critical endeavors.

8. Don't freak out about "failure." Stand up, dust off, start over, move forward.

9. Make your leadership development and personal growth a top priority by calendaring it. Do it now.

CHAPTER FIVE

Is Your Business Rotting? You Get What You Settle For!

Law #2, the law of operations states: every aspect of the business is systematized to efficiently and effectively meet stated goals through planning, policies, procedures, and measured performance.

"A system is a set of things, actions, ideas, and information that interact with each other, and in so doing, alter other systems," Michael E. Gerber writes in *The E-Myth Revisited*.

There's a myth among independent restaurateurs. It goes something like this: "Chain restaurants are successful because they have systems." But the reality is chain restaurants are successful because they use systems every day. We don't have to whine about what they have and we don't. We can create and implement systems just as they do. In fact, thanks to our smaller size and fewer bureaucratic hoops, independents are much more nimble and can systematize faster.

Systematizing your restaurant will help you elevate to a place where you can work on your business and not in it every day. For me and my family, systems development, implementation and refinement opened up new career paths and opportunities. I've been able to work now at the strategic level, write my book, consult for other independent restaurateurs, develop my websites, study leadership, hypnosis, and spirituality, hike on the beach, and take lots of pictures—all things I love to do. For Gary, he's been able to mostly retire (although he now says his job is to be my "roadie," which I also love!).

Shila, at the age of 27, is the highly skilled and competent president of five companies (including our management company), attends graduate school, is the mother of two-and-half-year-old twins, is pregnant with a third child, keeps up an active social life, even writes personal thank-you cards, and works out religiously. Chad is in college full-time, manages back-of-the-house operations, and is developing and refining back-of-the-house training and leadership systems. Don't forget he's also the dad of my grandtwins and the ultimate support system for our president. Systems, baby! Systems! *We'd all still be cooking and waiting tables without systems.*

ACTION LEADS TO SUCCESS

Robert Ringer, taking a cue from Einstein in naming his book *Action! Nothing Happens until Something Moves,* said,

"As the years have passed, I have increasingly zeroed in on action as the most important success habit when it comes to determining how an individual's life plays out."

Make something happen: Move toward systems immediately.

Start with your vision, goals. You decide what you want to accomplish on big things and little things. Write them down. Remember if it's not on your list, it doesn't exist. Make it exist—in writing. Planning is a process, a step toward implementation. It is action and offers accountability many independent restaurateurs lack. The fastest way to get to the bottom line in systems development is to ask the prime question: "What does success look like to me?"

This deceptively simple question can be applied to absolutely any aspect of your business—or life for that matter—and always delivers a sophisticated answer. Just like in falling in love, there's a fully sensual component here. Use all your senses. You could add: what does success taste like, smell like, sound like, feel like? Begin to really see; draw the big picture of success.

A proverb states, "She who asks the question cannot avoid the answer." Ask (and answer) as many questions as you can.

WRITE IT DOWN, COLOR IT UP

I make huge vision/planning boards out of butcher paper. My current one is nearly 12 feet long. I always "begin" on the far right of the page with the answer to the prime question. I use vibrant coloring markers to first draw the success picture. When the picture is clear, I work (draw, make notes, lists) step by step to the left, asking myself the prequels to the prime question: What had to happen the week before that? I write down, draw, make notes, and list what I know for sure and leave room to add things I realize as I go along. For example, I may know for sure I've got to get a loan, write a marketing plan, or recruit a partner. I continue then with what had to happen before that? I repeat this cycle till I'm at "today" with my success plan laid out in front of me. Sometimes my vision boards stay up on the wall for a whole year and often well past the time I've taken something from idea to reality.

It doesn't mean it's always perfect. Sometimes I have to cut or cover over a section if I change my mind or direction. Sometimes I have to start completely over from scratch. The process alone helps sharpen my vision and planning skills. Plus, it's fun!

"The odds of hitting your target go up dramatically when you aim at it," Mal Pancoast says. It's easier to aim at your target if you can see it. Post your target, your vision board, on your wall.

When I started systematizing the Squeeze, it seemed overwhelming with everything needing systematic upgrading. It was hard to figure out where to start, but I didn't allow the enormity of it to stop the forward progress.

Remember, the law of operations states: Every aspect of the business is systematized to efficiently and effectively meet stated goals through planning, policies, procedures, and measured performance. Each of the laws is interrelated and dependent on the others. What we didn't know we learned, and we vowed not to recreate the wheel as we hacked our way through our learning process. We built systems to facilitate each of the Five Irrefutable Laws of Restaurant Success:

- leadership
- operations
- financials
- products/services
- marketing

Each systematic upgrade cascaded into other upgrades.

A small example: Soda was served in cans, a quaint '70s holdover that wasn't really appealing for modern guests, accustomed to big sodas with refills. We installed a soda fountain system, requiring a better ice maker, an upgrade to the electrical system, new flooring, and a better floor drain, all of which necessitated a better cash flow system. Everything in the restaurant is part of the same living, breathing, organic system, each part related to the next. For ultimate success, each system must be healthy to support every other part. You might

> You might start out limping, but with systems development, you'll end up leaping!

start out limping, but with systems development, you'll end up leaping!

The Squeeze accepted cash only. We upgraded to take credit and debit cards. We had to install the physical system: phone and data lines, credit card swipe terminals, and printers. Accepting credit cards impacted other systems to the tune of about $2,500 in monthly credit-card company fees. We couldn't have made the shift if we hadn't been developing efficiency systems at the same time.

There was no inventory system, no monitoring of product coming in or going out, no waste sheets for product loss, burn, or spoilage. I had to build systems for paying invoices, preparing quarterly payroll, and sales and use tax returns, and processing paychecks. Many of the checklists and systems we created from scratch, all the while fine-tuning actually running the business. The good news was we would either sink or swim, and we were pretty good swimmers, even if we gasped and choked on water sometimes.

GETTING THE TOOLS YOU NEED–FAST

It took us many years to build our systems, but the good news for you is I've put together a comprehensive resource list through this book and on my website to help you make changes quickly.

At MistyYoung.com, you'll find a wide variety of resources and links to many free and some subscription sites. I didn't get here by myself, but with my family, guests, and associates backing me up, I've been able to really learn a tremendous amount. With the right training and resources from many restaurant industry experts, I've been blessed to collect valuable tools and expertise to propel me. You'll be able to drill down much further into my sources on the website.

PLANNING TO SUCCEED

You need a plan to be successful. Don't let that freak you out; planning isn't hard. Keep in mind that successful people have systems and *systems require planning.* With the answers to the prime question "What does success look like to me?" you're well on the way, once you can "see" the goal.

If you're already in business, business planning might seem unnecessary and you may even be thinking "plan is a four-letter word." So is hope. Businesses don't survive on hope, but you can stand on, monitor, adjust, upgrade, follow through, *and grow* with a plan.

A restaurant client recently said, "I can't afford the software and I can't pay you to develop my plan." The reality is a business owner is the right person to develop the business plan. It's your vision for the company. To develop a plan you don't have to have resources, just *resourcefulness.*

The U.S. Small Business Administration has just released a brand-new, comprehensive, free tool to write a business plan. The SBA's hold-your-hand tool will guide you through eight fill-in sections. You'll upload your logo or graphic, answer a series of questions, and end up with a solid business plan. You can start, stop, save and return and, when you're done, print! You could complete a very basic plan in a day, and continue to flesh it out with greater detail over a couple weeks. Close your office door and get at it! You can search it directly, or use my links to the SBA and other services and subscriptions over at MistyYoung.com. You don't have to know how to do everything. You just have to start by taking action. The universe loves speed. Ramp up!

In 2007, as we were preparing to open the first Reno location, I needed to develop a break-even analysis. I'm not really talented with tasks of that nature. Frankly, I love numbers and spreadsheets, but I like to get to the results. I don't really want to do all the programming details and formulas. Idea—to—results, I'm all about that. Details? No. Big picture? Yes! I finally found a downloadable, restaurant-specific, break-even spreadsheet, paid a low membership fee, and voilà, the tool was immediately in my hands. Of course, you can find more info on my website.

Not long after I became a member of an extensive restaurant resource site, I literally downloaded every single document from its huge download directory. Whether I needed it immediately or not, I wanted the library to help me develop my business. I spent the next five years working through the downloaded library, creating updated operations manuals, policies, and procedures, training handbooks, checklists, financial analysis tools, ticket timing evaluations, and much more.

Peter Drucker said, "What gets measured gets managed." I'd add to it, "What gets measured *and reported* gets managed *even better.*" We had this cycle: change, measure, track, report; change, measure, track, report …

BENEFITS OF A MARKETING SYSTEM

I suddenly began to receive outrageous marketing material from this seemingly crazy guy, Rory Fatt, about how to "put my marketing on autopilot" with all kinds of what seemed to be outlandish claims. I ordered an introductory package and never looked back. After a couple years in Rory's Platinum Plus restaurant industry mastermind group, we signed onto the marketing system that changed everything. It is the incredibly sophisticated program powering our customized EggHead Breakfast Club. While I've introduced you briefly to the program, I'd like to give you a more detailed overview. Find a comprehensive case study at MistyYoung.com. We've been members of Rory's group for years now and find it to be one of the most strategic and profitable decisions we've made.

Rory taught us to take action in marketing. His marketing-is-math philosophy teaches his clients to prepare, test, market, measure, and start over again. We followed his guidance, learned what worked for us, discarded what didn't, and kept building our marketing system.

In *Action! Nothing Happens Until Something Moves,* Ringer said. "Action converts an idea into an experience.

Action creates reality." Our action created a whole new reality for us: a marketing system with reliable results, a way to reach our beloved EggHeads with relevant information and offers they opted in to receive. Marketing guru Dan Kennedy says, "When your clients ask to hear from you, you become a welcome guest instead of an annoying pest" in their lives. We much prefer welcome-guest status!

The EggHead Breakfast Club is powered by a comprehensive and sophisticated program, but is very easy to use. Merchants log in to a detailed dashboard, stocked with evaluation tools, dozens of analytical reports; scientific data presented in graphic format; free e-mail campaigns that can be run in a few simple steps to send offers, e-mail newsletters, updates, and so on; demographic and psychographic profiles; transaction information; and downloadable member lists. Ready-to-go, direct-mail postcard and letter campaigns can be launched with a push of a button. It's safe to say we've found an excellent marketing system.

One superbenefit is the daily survey. More than one EggHead reading this book will say, "I recognize that!" Based on criteria we've set and can adjust, an automatic survey is e-mailed out to guests who have dined with us that day. Guest responses help us identify problems, superstars, and trends. We have found the daily surveys to be a great training tool and associate-praise delivery system! We've even incorporated the survey results into a $48,000, manager annual bonus incentive pool.

One additional benefit as we systematized our marketing was the creation of our custom newsletter. The EggHead EggZaminer (thank you Shila for the great name!) has been in print now for almost five years. Archives of the print newsletter are available through my website at the bottom of the page. We use the innovative reporting functions to identify up to 3,500 guest households to receive our monthly printed newsletter (which we also deliver by e-mail to all EggHeads). The EggZaminer is a strategic tool to keep our members involved with us and up to date on specials and family information, and to offer promotions. We always have testimonials, or, as we call them, "guestimonials" in our newsletter too. These genuine, kind, loving *permission-based* testimonials come right out of our guest surveys and program enrollment form. Yes, we ask for comments, and we ask for permission to use them in our marketing. Thank you EggHeads!

There are many components of this program: from birthday and anniversary postcards to award letters; free e-mail campaigns and paid multiphase, direct-mail postcard campaigns; the incredible detail, tracking, and ability to completely customize the program to our brand and image. We've been thrilled with all of it and we have a strong allegiance to our colleagues in Rory's Platinum Plus mastermind group with whom we share great ideas and successes. I love the program so much that I serve as a marketing agent. Rory and I have created a 40-minute, deeply detailed introduction to the program that you can view at www.mistysmarketing-discovery.com. The program isn't just for restaurants either;

there are all kinds of businesses using this sophisticated loyalty program as the foundation of their marketing success.

LOYALTY PROGRAMS WORK

Food-service-industry consulting firm Technomic has completed research on loyalty programs. Their findings include:

> Fifty-eight percent of loyalty-club members say they are likely to base their where-to-dine decision on whether they have a membership at that brand.

> Of the consumers who say they currently participate in loyalty marketing programs, membership is higher among casual-dining brands (57 percent) than fast-casual brands (44 percent).

> Seventy-seven percent of loyalty members say e-mail is the preferred method for receiving rewards communications.

> A vast majority (96 percent) of participants in rewards programs say they have visited a restaurant associated with their membership within the past six months.

Consumers are concerned about privacy. Seventy percent say they would be more inclined to sign up for a rewards program if they could be guaranteed that the restaurant would not pass along their information.

It's very clear loyalty programs can benefit independent restaurants if done well. Ours is done exceptionally well—more info at the website.

You've got to take action. You're in charge. You get to decide. It's in your hands. It's your choice whether your business succeeds or fails. Get moving, not just theoretically, but physically too. Move your body.

Jerry Seinfeld said, "To me, if life boils down to one thing, it's movement. To live is to keep moving." If you're hung over, obese, and physically inactive, what does that say for your brain, for your mental ability? Move your body, affect your brain. With a sharper brain, you're going to have more confidence to move toward competence, what psychologists refer to as the competence/confidence loop. You get better at something, you're more confident; you're more confident, you take bigger chances, you get better. You see the pattern.

Confidence/Competence Loop

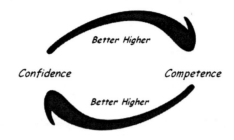

Better Higher

Confidence   Competence

Better Higher

Dr. Bruce Lipton states we change our bodies through our environment and we change our environment with our thoughts. He literally says, "Evolution can happen this afternoon!" We create our biology with our belief.

As an advocate for health in all areas, I know first-hand the value of movement. But movement without order is a recipe for disaster. Here's how I do it: I set my course, decide what I want to accomplish and give some order to my thoughts. Then I move, putting the plan in motion allowing my physiology to affect my psychology. Many portions of this book were dictated from a Bluetooth headset while I worked out on an elliptical trainer in my office. Writer's block? Not when I'm sweating! Business block? Order your thoughts, get moving, take action, defeat chaos. Read books, download and study personal growth and human potential resources, develop your own leadership and begin to develop others. As you get better, you begin to get "in shape" and, from a

> Order your thoughts, get moving, take action, defeat chaos.

healthy place, you have a much stronger likelihood of meeting your goals and increasing your opportunity to serve your family, business, associates, and community.

ROTTING? YOU GET WHAT YOU SETTLE FOR

Nevada attorney general Frankie Sue Del Papa used to tell me, "You get what you settle for." I realized later it's a fairly well-known quote, but I heard it from her first.

I say the same to you: You get what you settle for. If your business is rotting, if it's stagnating, if it's not moving forward, you've settled for that. You've allowed that to happen. I know that can hurt. The truth is you get to decide whether you're moving forward on a path of progression and improvement or whether you're accepting things as they are.

Don't accept things as they are if you're unhappy and know you can improve them. If you're not refining, you're declining! On the same note, if you're stoked, you're doing all you need to, that's great! If you need to improve, reading this book is fantastic action you've already taken but don't let it stop on these pages. Implement the "Ingredients for Success" at the end of each chapter, and over at mistyyoung. com. These are useful, proven, valuable, business-building *action steps*.

THE ANSWER IS: BETTER QUESTIONS

In today's culture, solo is old school. Social is new school. Ask for help. It's everywhere and it's easily accessible. Start with questions. Think "we" first. Your associates are some of the most valuable people in your business. They will help if you ask them.

Remember, don't settle. Ask a lot of questions. It's what we talked about earlier. When you fell in love with someone, when you fell in love with your business, when you were lying in bed at night dreaming about owning your little restaurant, you asked a lot of questions. What if the menu … what if the dining room … what if I had a full house and I was the only person on the floor or on the line? What if I didn't know how to do something? Well, then you had to ask new questions. Well, if I don't know the answer to that question? What if I did know? Then what would the answer be?

I'm paraphrasing world-renowned, personal-development leader, speaker and author, Anthony Robbins, who says, "If you ask yourself a question and you don't know the answer, don't settle for that. When the answer is 'I don't know,' ask the follow-up, which is, 'Well, if I did know, what would the answer be?'" This line of questioning works not only on yourself, but as you also work to develop people, when they say "I don't know," follow up with, "Well, if you did know, what do you suppose the answer could be?" It's exciting to see answers start popping when you use this tool.

I have used this questioning technique successfully for years in my restaurants, and my personal life, and with coaching clients. I start with the prime question: what does success look like to you? It could look like a, b, c, and d. But if I don't know, I'm just going to start winging it. Robert Ringer says, "Action is the key to the brain's ignition." I've found the same to be true in my own experience. Sometimes you just have to leap to make the answer appear. You can sit on the fence forever, but all you get is a swollen behind.

Here are Robert Ringer's Ten Never-Fail Rules of Success:

Rule No. 1: Ask.
Rule No. 2: Ask again.
Rule No. 3: Ask again.
Rule No. 4: Ask again.
Rule No. 5: Ask again.
Rule No. 6: Ask again.
Rule No. 7: Ask again.
Rule No. 8: Ask again.
Rule No. 9: Ask again.
Rule No. 10: Ask again.

Questions are the answer. And all of us know how to ask questions. We have to ask and keep asking and refining for better questions, and then digging deeper to get better answers. Find the answer to your business question. You likely already know it.

Here's another great starter: What are three action steps you are currently aware of, that, if taken, would move you closer to your goal?

The key here is you're already aware of them; you already know what to do! Do them! What *would* you do? What *could* you do? What *should* you do? Do it! Start where you are. You don't have to know how to do everything; you just have to know the next couple steps. If you're driving across the country, you can't see the whole road at once. You make the trip mile by mile. Your answers get you to the goal step by step.

You'll find an article I wrote called, "10 Great Questions for Restaurant Renewal," on my website. Read it to start asking and answering very specific questions today. Then take action. You'll also find my Set the Expectation formula and checklist to help you make some immediate progress.

You have to start moving in the right direction, and asking questions is the best way to do it. Keep asking questions. Ask questions about marketing, cooking, guest service times, about consistency, financial performance, training, your maintenance schedule, your vendors, your prices, cost of goods sold, your prime cost. Question everything; settle for nothing. Don't be stagnant; keep moving forward. Build your systems and make them strong.

> You have to start moving in the right direction, and asking questions is the best way to do it.

Having systems was absolutely key to my being on the air with Bobby Flay and being covered so frequently in the news. Without systems and my constant attention to them, I would not have been able to immediately answer the Food Network or Melinda Emerson's questions for the *New York Times*. I know my statistics, my projections, and metrics. I asked questions continuously throughout my systems development phase. Some of the best answers came from my associates and guests, and we'll talk about that soon enough. Meanwhile, let's dig into numbers.

INGREDIENTS FOR SUCCESS

1. Move. Toward systems. Your body.
2. Answer the prime question in writing: "What does success look like to me?"
3. Draw a vision board; make it lively and colorful (see samples at website).
4. Write a basic plan. The prime question and vision board are great starting tools.
5. Start measuring everything in your restaurant. What gets measured gets managed.
6. Sign up for a loyalty program. Don't wait; this is mission critical.
7. Ask more questions; get more answers.
8. Download "10 Great Questions for Restaurant Renewal" from my website.

CHAPTER SIX

Defeat the Dreaded Restaurant Owner Disease: FTI Syndrome

Successful restaurants are built on the Five Irrefutable Laws of Restaurant Success, beginning at the top of the STAR, with you, in developing and refining your leadership, your personal growth and accountability, and that of your associates. You can't stand on broken feet, but as you develop a solid footing of operations and financials, you can then deliver excellent products/services, and marketing that works.

Law #2, the law of operations: every aspect of the business is systematized to efficiently and effectively meet stated goals through policies, procedures, and measured performance.

The law is straightforward. It doesn't say, "It's a good idea to systematize," or "You might consider planning." It says *the business IS systematized with stated goals and measurement.* We can't be successful without focusing on every operational detail.

Operations is the sweet spot for most independent restaurant owners. We know how to do this; it's the safe zone, the fall-back position, the place we're comfortable. We went into this business for our love of it, right? We know how to cook, how to serve, how to please guests and hit the center of the target with excellent food, beverages, and a fantastic, hospitable experience. That's all great, but what about those other pesky operational and financial considerations such as inventory management, kitchen timing, recipe costing, portion control, waste management, pricing for profitability, service standards, health and safety, security, menu development, recruiting—it can seem overwhelming, can't it? It doesn't have to be.

OPERATIONS ON THE FAST TRACK

Operational soundness is all the stuff unseen by the guest, the transparent, behind-the-scenes activities that make your restaurant great. We talked about systems development in the last chapter. Operations is where the rubber meets the road. In the case of the Squeeze, we standardized everything. We never would have been able to expand without standardization. If you have no desire to grow or expand, that's fine. You may just want to stabilize your existing restaurant, making it easier to operate, fall in love with it again, take a vacation, move your succession plan forward, elevate your family members to take over, or perhaps sell it. Whatever your goal, systematizing operations must be the number-one priority to helping you realize your goals.

Getting out of your comfort zone, trying new things takes time. Restaurant expert, David Scott Peters said, "Anything you do for the first few times takes longer. But after you have mastered the task, it becomes quick and easy. The only way to get better at it is to do it.

Remember that line about "chains are successful because they *use* systems every day?" You can be too. Over and over I've heard coaching clients say they need help being accountable. They may have an idea of "what" to do but don't know "how" to do it or what order to do it in. So, without accountability, they give up. They don't move forward and no one is there to hold them accountable.

Although well intentioned, they back down into the comfort of serving or cooking. All the while, the little details are nagging at them. Yes, I worked days, nights, weekends, and holidays. Yes, it was exhausting. Yes, it was ultimately successful. You can benefit from all that time, by taking this secret recipe and creating operational systems on fast track. I was accountable for getting it done. You can be too. You've got to develop your leadership daily, not in a day. Start building your operational success with checklists. This stuff isn't rocket science, but a systematized process with a structured timeline will be your best friend as you move forward to develop and fall in love with the business of your dreams.

DON'T BE SICK, CHOOSE HEALTH

The "disease" that keeps many independent restaurateurs from moving forward is the dreaded FTI Syndrome. Have you heard of it? Failure To Implement Syndrome just means you know what needs to be done, but you fail to do it. With enthusiasm and energy, encouragement and accountability, you can achieve your dreams and defeat the deadly FTI Syndrome.

> You can achieve your dreams and defeat the deadly FTI Syndrome.

It was true for me. To hack your next 90 days of action, take leadership by building the systems and processes listed below. This ambitious Restaurant Reboot list (with a nod to industry expert Joe Erickson) is the same basic structure I use to help my clients move from limping to leaping. (Find a printable copy on the website.)

- Begin to build your guest database.
- Implement a daily calendaring system for your leadership and personal growth and development. (If it's not on your list, it doesn't exist!)
- Implement a daily summary report (likely available in your point-of-sale (POS) system).
- Implement a daily manager's log.
- Schedule weekly meetings with managers and associates.

- Establish guest service minimums. (Leave nothing to chance!)
- Write standardized job descriptions with built-in accountability for all positions.
- Create an employee handbook (include job descriptions above).
- Create opening and closing checklists for every position in both front and back of the house.
- Create an organization chart with built-in accountability standards.
- Update and review your prime cost numbers daily; prepare weekly and monthly reports.
- Begin tracking key inventory items (select/track up to 15 items on a trial basis).
- Track item sales mix using POS reports.
- Create a labor budget to develop schedules, and schedule on performance not seniority.
- Implement daily prep sheets; establish par prep levels.
- Implement par purchase levels.
- Take monthly, or even weekly, inventory. (Be adamant about this!)
- Migrate your chart of accounts to the Uniform System of Accounts for Restaurants.
- Migrate to weekly inventory process (what gets measured gets managed).
- Implement a digital tracking process for prime cost.

Prime cost is your total food and beverage costs (cost of goods sold) plus payroll expenses as a percentage of sales in a period. The more frequently you calculate prime cost, the better your ratio will be. We measure prime cost daily, weekly, monthly, quarterly, and annually, and we compare store to store and period to period. We're kind of fanatical about it as prime cost has proven to be an indisputable analytical tool and easy to calculate and understand by our entire tribe. Your prime cost should run no higher than 60–65 percent of total sales in a table service restaurant and 55–60 percent in quick service (general rules of thumb). We shoot for 50-55%.

I won't try in our limited space here to go into each of these in extreme detail; you get the idea. There's a boatload of work to be done. It can feel overwhelming. It doesn't have to be. You can be supported in your effort. I'm willing to help you. There are also many, many other industry groups and experts willing to help you. Some are free. Many are inexpensive. Others are moderate. All are valuable. *I have massive resources over at MistyYoung.com and provide a wealth of free content and links to help you immediately.*

The late, great Zig Ziglar said, "You will get all you want in life if you help enough other people get what they want." Thank you, Zig!

I'm blessed to have energy, enthusiasm, and personal interest in being helpful, kind, and courteous. I live with my mantra question every day, "How may I serve?" and follow up, of course, with "What is my truth?" I ask and answer these questions daily.

I stand in my truth, to be of service, to be healthy on the physical, emotional, mental, social, professional, and spiritual levels, and to assist as many others as I can to achieve health and happiness in their life and business. Thank you for being on this journey with me! Let's end independent restaurant failure. Let's be doctors of FTI Syndrome and let's work together to get healthy!

You're poisoned with FTI syndrome! Take a huge daily dose of the only known remedy!

HACKING FINANCIALS: THE LONG HAUL

Before digging into the law in detail, here's an important concept: Restaurateurs don't succeed in the long run by skimming cash, paying under the table, or otherwise operating unethically. I'm willing to bet that's not you, but many of our friendly competitors do business exactly as such. I don't. I think integrity matters.

Law #3: the law of financials: with integrity and diligence, financials and products are tracked, monitored, and adjusted to assure financial health, fitness, and profitability.

While developing operations through systematizing, it was clear I needed help in the area of financials if we were to become the strong company I envisioned. In 2006 I hired a consultant to help me navigate and better understand Quick-Books and create more accurate reporting. I struggled as I continued to learn. After two years, it was clear I had reached my maximum potential (and interest) in managing financials, and we had grown to the point an internal, full-time controller (and knot untier) was needed.

As the company continued to grow and our financials and tax accounting became even more complex, we morphed again, to a full time internal accountant, and an outsourced chief financial officer. My son-in-law, Chad, coined a phrase I love, "tell me what to do and I'll do it," which is what I now say regularly to our CFO. Our CFO has helped us develop budgets with built-in break-even analyses, variance measures, and comparisons. We've moved light years ahead in a very short time.

I appreciate former restaurant certified public accountant and renowned industry expert Jim Laube for his brilliance and plain speaking in the area of restaurant finance. More on Jim and his awesome resources and expertise can be found at MistyYoung.com.

Financial reporting provides the true fundamental measurement of restaurant health. Using the three most common forms of restaurant financial reporting, you can quickly identify a healthy restaurant, or diagnose with tools and information to treat an unhealthy restaurant. The basics are: the profit and loss statement (P&L), the balance sheet, and the cash flow statement.

Whole books are written about restaurant financials, and I don't profess to be an expert on this topic. You know my drill, though. I'm an excellent student and know where to get information and whom to ask questions of. We'll take a look at each of three reports to underscore their importance and how to use them effectively in your business.

PROFIT AND LOSS STATEMENT = KNOWLEDGE

First off, many independent restaurateurs don't have what I call a healthy fixation on the numbers, and if they do, they may be unwisely focused on the top or bottom line, paying scant attention to the details in between. But the middle of the P&L is where the real golden nuggets of information live, the place you can turn to when you need to stop the bleeding—or pay bonuses and incentives!

The P&L, also referred to as an income statement shows your gross sales; your variable expenses such as food and beverage costs and total labor costs (together, these are called prime cost); your fixed expenses, which remain fairly constant, such as your lease or mortgage, utilities, taxes, marketing, and general expenses, and ends with net income at the bottom line.

As a tool, the P&L is unbeatable in identifying trends, opportunities, and problems. *If you're preparing financials yourself, unless you're a CPA, stop it right now.* Just stop. I know who you are. This is what you say, "I can't afford a CPA or a CFO. I'm getting what I need." Right. You don't see your financials by the fifth of the month just closed; you don't have your prime cost weekly; your inventory isn't done; you don't have waste information; you don't have the backup records; but you're going to get it all done someday when you have time. *Quit wasting precious time and human energy and upgrade this mission-critical system immediately. Hire a professional.*

One of my coaching clients recently said, "Why do I have to create a budget and do all this reporting? Other restaurant owners I know don't do any of it and they're doing fine, with three houses and vacations and plenty of cash. We're struggling." The reality is you don't have to do any of this. You should want to do it. A reminder: businesses paying employees under the table, skimming from the top, under-reporting sales, and cheating on taxes aren't healthy either physically or spiritually. Dishonesty might pay off in the short term but doesn't ultimately lead to success. Besides that, "white collar crime" can result in prison. That's not the vacation I have in mind!

Managing restaurant financials is not brain surgery, but it does require a specific set of skills and precise thinking.

Hire a qualified CPA so you can focus on other aspects of your business such as developing your leadership, operations, products/services, and marketing. Most independent restaurateurs aren't financial experts. In fact, restaurateurs who are experts at operations *and* financials consistently outperform others without the same skill set. Are you an expert at both? Neither am I. Hire the expertise you need, understand what you need to know, and leverage both to success.

In my professional development, it has taken me years to get to a deeper understanding of the financial aspects of running a restaurant. As law #3, the law of financials, states: "With integrity and diligence, financials and products are tracked, monitored, and adjusted to assure financial health, fitness, and profitability." For us, it was the final piece of the puzzle, when it should have been one of the first.

"The difference between well-managed companies and not-so-well-managed companies is the degree of attention they pay to the numbers," said Harold Geneen, former chairman, ITT Corporation. Energy goes where attention flows, so send your attention to the numbers. Give your energy, enthusiasm, and intelligence and watch the dramatic changes you can make in your business as it begins to blossom under your new financial leadership.

Industry expert Jim Laube says, "The restaurant business is about people and food and the cold hard reality of facts, figures and finances." The importance of accurate, detailed information that is understood and used cannot be overstated. Great food and service rarely take a restaurant down.

Poor financial management and controls, indicating a lack of leadership, are the usual suspects in restaurant failure. That's why leadership is the first law. The more you know and understand about the financial aspects of your restaurant, the more likely you are to achieve your goals.

BALANCE SHEET SHOWS FINANCIAL HEALTH

The next basic financial report, the balance sheet, can be thought of as a snapshot or a scoreboard, and I've also heard it referred to as a "slice of cake," essentially representing one tiny piece of the whole, or a moment in time. The balance sheet provides a clear picture of your financial situation *in the moment*. It is an impressive and useful tool for improvement and growth. The balance sheet compares your assets (what you own) to your liabilities (what you owe) with the difference between the two being your "net worth," or "equity." Remember the balance sheet is always a snapshot, and the look of it can change substantially if your business is seasonal, or because of other factors such as high product inventory on hand (why would you accept this?), or recent large expenditures such as that new $12,000 pizza oven.

Many companies look at a balance sheet annually. We look at ours at least monthly. It's not always pretty, but on a regular basis we're able to make adjustments in the moment as the balance sheet is an in-the-moment, snapshot tool helping our financial stability. We make it our business to stay on top of our financial reports, not wanting to give up working cash in the bank for product sitting on a shelf. I'd rather pay payroll than have 25 cases of champagne on hand because it was a good deal (as much as I love champagne!).

"The balance sheet is the company's thermometer. It lets you know whether you're healthy or not. The P&L tells you how you got that way and what you can do about it," says Jack Stack in his *Great Game of Business.*

At the Squeeze, we've recently migrated our entire chart of accounts system to follow the Uniform System of Accounts for Restaurants (USAR), which allows us to better track and monitor our numbers against industry averages. This is an important benchmarking tool. We know it's strategic to emulate successful operators and to keep an eagle eye on ratios, expenses, and trends. It's part of what's helped us grow during a recession.

CASH FLOW: WHERE IT ALL GOES

Finally, the cash flow statement: This analytical tool helps you identify if your cash is flowing like a river current, stagnating in a pond, or meandering along in a pathetic stream. It's a great planning tool to use to project out into the future when particular bills come due and not spend up everything on hand right now.

Smart operators also use financial statements to work in a partnership with key suppliers. Here's the deal, if you make money, they make money, share your info, seek their advice and counsel! Your suppliers want you to succeed. We partner with Sysco—a global leader in selling, marketing and distributing food products to restaurants. Sysco has proven to be a strategic and valuable cost control *and profit driving* ally. Set up a meeting with your Sysco rep, ask tons of questions, and don't look back.

Much of this seems so elementary, doesn't it? Sort of like, "Well, yeah!" But the fact of the matter is many independent restaurateurs—I'd dare say most—don't have a good handle on their financials. Without excellent financial controls, you're definitely not on the hack track to success. I'm thrilled where the Squeeze is now with our level of sophistication and detailed information, but I'm bummed how long it took us to get here. Alas, I don't have energy for regret.

> But the fact of the matter is many independent restaurateurs—I'd dare say most—don't have a good handle on their financials.

From links to excellent resources and articles, including downloads, of course, there's a ton more over at my website.

Meanwhile, take the only known antidote for FTI syndrome (action!) and get moving toward your compliance with the law of operations and the law of financials. You'll want to get your associates in on the action too. As you develop your leadership and begin to seriously shape up your company, your associates will become your most important allies in living to the letter of the laws.

INGREDIENTS FOR SUCCESS

1. Write down three ideas to tune up operational efficiency. If you don't know, ask the question, "Well, if I did know, what would they be?"
2. Decide right now that you'll be accountable to yourself. Commit to it. Recruit an accountability partner if need be.
3. Take the only known antidote to FTI syndrome, action, right away. Don't stay sick by choice. Reading a book isn't enough.
4. Hack your next 90 days of success by implementing the Restaurant Reboot list, starting today (printable version from website).
5. Hire an accountant, a CPA, a CFO. Stop "trying," start getting it done.
6. Regularly review and understand your three basic financial reports.
7. Get your associates in on the action; start by communicating your goals.

CHAPTER SEVEN

Add a Pinch of Magic to Your Recipe

The successful restaurateur doesn't think "me" first but "we" first. Your well-trained associates are your face to your guests, vendors, and community. Replicating yourself successfully is worth every moment it takes to make it happen.

> Replicating yourself successfully is worth every moment it takes to make it happen.

According to law #4, the law of products/services, our products must be reliable and we must diligently serve our customers and associates with courtesy, appreciation, respect, and kindness.

When we bought the restaurant, I kept saying that the most important thing was the guest, the guest, the guest. I hammered all the time on the guest, and of course, the guest is the most important thing, right? *Not so.* Successful restaurateurs realize the value of happy associates to create a happy guest experience. The triangle of strength is: well-trained, happy associates; thrilled guests; safe, clean, healthy restaurant. Each side of the triangle needs the others to be balanced and stable. One part weak or missing and the whole thing faces collapse.

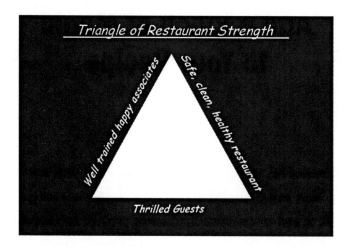

Triangle of Restaurant Strength

Well trained happy associates

Safe, clean, healthy restaurant

Thrilled Guests

Early on, I had been hammering on process, systems, efficiency, and I could see family and associates rolling their eyes as if to say, "Oh my God, does she think about nothing else?"

The truth is, I really didn't think of much else. I worked on processes, systems, and efficiencies all day and then lay awake at night thinking about it. I kept a notebook and pen by my bed (until the iPhone came out). I would get up in the middle of the night and write ideas, and I was always focused on how we could make it better. Every day I asked, how we could make it better—always asking and answering questions. I've mentioned how my business partner Chad helped me change my perspective from processes, systems, and efficiency, to *people*, systems, and efficiency, but I haven't told you about the aha moment. It was a beautiful transition, but the event itself was quite ugly.

It was Father's Day, 2007. I was working in the restaurant. It was crazy busy from the get go. One of the guys in the kitchen said something crappy to me, and I snapped something crappy right back to him. Without another word, he gave me the one-finger salute, took off his apron, and walked out. I put on an apron, and I got in that corner, and I cooked 178 omelettes myself that day.

On Father's Day, one of our busiest days of the year, I was thoroughly exhausted at closing time. I went home that night and folded myself up in the corner of the bed in a fetal position. It was not easy. It was immediately clear to me, employees are not labor units, and I understood at the deepest possible level the importance of respect, appreciation, and kindness for my associates. As often happens in my life, I got the lesson now. I saw the magic, I shifted in the moment.

I recently toured our newest location on a very busy Sunday. I stepped through the kitchen, and I looked down the cooking line as these guys were pumping out an incredible volume of breakfasts. I said, "Guys, thank you so much. You're doing a great job." In the middle of the Sunday morning mayhem, one of the guys stopped and looked me square in the eye. He put out his hands toward me and said, "No. Thank you. *Thank you* for preparing and making jobs for us and for being such a cool boss." Yes, this actually happened.

It was awesome. It brought tears to my eyes, and I kept repeating, "Thank you." Ultimately, when you think about your associates as people and how important they are, you realize that it's not all about the guests. Yes, the guests are crucial, but the guests are going to have a sucky experience if your associates are having a sucky experience. People. *People* first. People, systems, and efficiencies.

MISSION STATEMENTS

The mission statement at the Squeeze In reflects our shift in attitude toward our associates. Our original mission statement was exclusively focused on the guests. Here's what our new one says.

> The Squeeze In delivers an extraordinary guest *and associate* experience through consistently prepared fresh high-quality food served in a safe, clean, fun environment with a focus on genuine guest service and community involvement.

I learned recently about "distilled mission statements," which are statements everyone can memorize. Here is our mission statement distilled:

> *"Squeeze In: great food and service every time for every guest; associates and community who care and are cared for."*

It's not hard to write a mission (or "promise") statement. Just decide what you stand for and write it down!

YOU GOTTA CHECK THE CHECKER WHO CHECKS THE CHECKER

How do we assure an extraordinary associate experience? We do it through our highly sophisticated training system. We realized as our company started growing that Misty, Gary, Shila, Chad, daughter Kay, nephew Rickey, and niece Amanda—whom we lovingly called the A-Team—could no longer serve each guest personally. I have superfond memories of the early days when we were the entire front-of-the-house contingent, rocking the Squeeze literally from sunrise until beer thirty.

Still, we had to assure every single guest was getting the kind of attention and care and love that we could personally give. We had to create a training system to do that. As previously mentioned, our training system includes checklists, individual position manuals, job descriptions, code of business conduct, and a series of nine videos. We require all potential candidates to watch and sign off on the videos before they even get a chance to show their stuff in a live audition on the floor. That's the best way we know to provide an exceptional guest experience while evaluating a potential associate at the same time. We also run regular workshops covering topics such as the EggHead Breakfast Club, excellent guest service, suggesting menu items or offering upgrades, even how to make our signature Bloody Marys. Of course, every training begins with a live-in-person orientation and a checklist.

This is a very specific orientation. Not just walking the candidate around the restaurant.

No, our orientation program tells the trainer what to show potential new associates, where to show them, sign off, check that everything's checked. The manuals are signed off and acknowledged, the process checked and double-checked. We like to say, "You gotta check the checker who checks the checker," meaning it has to be checked and verified by checking again. Our guests and associates are too important to be lost in shoddy training. That might seem to be overkill for a mom-and-pop restaurant—right?

It's not. Accountable training is 100 percent necessary in today's competitive environment. In the *Food Service Professional Guide to Waiter & Waitress Training*, author Lora Arduser says,

> While you may be the leader in your food service organization, you can't do everything. Consideration for one's colleagues and cooperation create a more productive environment, especially when working circumstances are particularly demanding. Working and thinking as a team helps to create an environment of collaboration, which will help to ensure your restaurant's ability to make profits. Teamwork can increase your pro-

ductivity, improve decision making, maximize the use of your human resources and make better use of your inventory. Make problem solving an automatic function of daily work, by team training.

Accountable training mattered when it was time for our associates to be the face of Squeeze In to our hundreds of thousands of guests. I couldn't do it anymore. Shila couldn't do it anymore, neither could Chad, Gary, Kay, Rickey, or other family members we'd had on the team over the years. We had to count on other folks, our trusted associates. We had to train them to serve as if we were serving the guests ourselves.

GREAT TRAINING SHOWS UP IN GUEST SURVEYS

In our daily guest surveys, our guest satisfaction rating rarely dips below 95 percent, combining good and excellent categories. This tells me our guests are happy, getting the kind of service they and I expect.

In your own restaurant it's a good thing to talk about your people, systems, and efficiencies, and how you're monitoring them. Family and associates laughingly accused me of being a ten-cent manager, a title I gladly embraced. They always appreciated it, though, when I "did the math" because then they could see why I had a healthy fixation on the numbers.

For example, in a breakfast restaurant an order of pancakes typically comes with butter, right? Whipped butter runs roughly 13 cents an ounce and a serving is a one-ounce soufflé cup. I realized our associates were serving a towering heap of butter twice the size of the one-ounce soufflé cup, doubling our cost. Half the time, the guest didn't eat the extra butter, and it was thrown into a bus tray.

Now, one ounce of whipped butter thrown in the bus tray costs 13 cents times 21 throwaways ($2.73) per restaurant per day (4 x $2.73 = $10.92) times 363 days per year and it comes out to a whopping $3,963.96 at the end of the year in overfilled, thrown-away butter. That's just *one item* on the menu. What gets wasted, thrown away, or overserved in your restaurant? You know how to find out? Go through your bus trays and trashcans! I know it sounds gross, but you've got to have a healthy fixation on the numbers if you've got any chance at making a living in the restaurant business.

Personally, I don't like buying food, paying someone to prepare and serve it, and then throwing it away. I can't stand that. I absolutely don't like waste. I let my associates know we've got to take the butter cup and shave it off right across the top. Use your little rubber spatula and after you fill up the butter cup, shave it off to make it level. Don't put so much out there that you're going to throw it away. They want more? Bring them more! But let's not automatically set up for waste. Waste is arrogance, which isn't very conducive to good business.

Whipped Butter = 13 cents an ounce
x 21 throwaways on average each day = $2.73
x 4 restaurants = $10.92
x 363 days a year of butter thrown away =
$3,963.96

The guests benefit when you look at the trash. On several bus-tray analyses we also discovered a tremendous amount of uneaten toast. Our omelettes were served with two slices of expensive honey wheatberry toast, cut into triangles for four pieces. We found tons of toast in the trash. We decided to make a shift: bottomless toast for all breakfasts. The key was omelettes would now be served with a single slice of toast, cut into two triangles. The guest could have as much as they wanted. Making the change from automatically serving toast to be tossed to toast that was eaten reduced our bread usage and cost dramatically to the point we were able to contract with a local gourmet bakery that created a custom, preservative-free wheat bread to our specifications. That bakery also got our entire bread account across all four restaurants. Custom, preservative-free bread? One more indication of a high-end breakfast restaurant.

What other "small" things can you think of? Lemons? Salsa? Poorly trimmed vegetables? Bread heels? Can't those be made into homemade croutons? Informed, accountable training makes the ultimate difference between waste and want. As we grew to nearly a hundred associates, we had to come up with an even more efficient training approach.

> Informed, accountable training makes the ultimate difference between waste and want.

THE FORMAT PROGRAM

We created an innovative, in-depth program we call Format, which you may also think of as an offsite manager's retreat. We thank Gary for the name. For a couple years he had been suggesting we build a Format for our managers to help them more fully understand our systems and the importance of efficiency. He knew it was critically important, and I knew what a huge project he was asking us to create. Shila and I took the years of training materials we had already developed, revised, and upgraded, and published a new comprehensive system for managers, complete with our Partnering for Performance program built right in. Format was born.

Designed initially for front-of-the-house general managers, it has now been expanded with sessions for the back of the house, and is held twice a year. Format is a multiday, off-site, high-level, intensive training program with incentives, fun, plenty of food and drink, surprises, and a whole lot of detailed business training. Shila and I worked together to design and deliver the initial program, which was received enthusiastically by our team.

For the first Format, we took the managers off-site to the Oregon coast for four days. They didn't know what to expect and were pretty leery at the beginning. By the end, they were sold. "When's the next event? We can't wait!"

The second was held at a beautiful resort in South Lake Tahoe, Nevada. We've held Format at an amazing vacation mansion in historic downtown Truckee, California, and even right here in Reno, with day trips to Sacramento. We've done role plays, cooking demonstrations, financial reviews, speed masterminding, kitchen tours, team-building exercises, consumed too much food and drink (going out to eat, conducting detailed review and scoring of other restaurants is part of the structured curriculum), hired guest presenters and private yoga instructors, and more. We build generous bonuses into the program and strive to make Format a perk, not a prison.

At Format, the managers go through an intensive financial review comparing restaurant to restaurant. Upon arrival, each receives a comprehensive binder with all kinds of financial reports from our point-of-sale and accounting systems. Guest averages, profit-and-loss statements, balance sheets, prime cost reports and detailed records on individual server performance. They see clock-in times and clock-out times and they review overtime and cost of goods sold in their location. Every manager can see percentage of sales by omelette and other entrees, and by alcoholic and nonalcoholic beverages. They see voids, comps, mistakes, problems. The financial review is always the thing they are most interested in. Turns out managers want to have a healthy fixation on numbers too!

Minutes are money. Clocking in prior to shift start can cost the company a huge amount. Let's say your overall average house wage is $12. In our case, with four locations and 85 hourly workers (some are on salary) the minutes add up fast. If each associate clocks in just five minutes before his/her shift officially begins...

$12/60 minutes = 20 cents a minute
5 minutes early x 85 associates = 425 minutes
daily (this is going to be bad!)
425 minutes x .20 = $85 daily
$85 daily x 363 days per year = $30,855 annually
before payroll taxes!

Minutes are money! A healthy fixation on the numbers requires you to manage minutes!

You need every tool you can get your hands on to manage operations and financials. Most restaurants today have a point-of-sale system. If not, it should be a top priority for your business. A POS system is one of the most important tools you could install immediately to help identify accurate prime cost, labor costs, food cost percentages, and to assist with scheduling. A POS system easily identifies opportunities to increase sales and take underperforming or unprofitable items off the menu.

Minutes are money! A healthy fixation on the numbers requires you to manage minutes!

At Format, we give the managers presentations and bring in interesting, relevant guest speakers. We give them incentives such as the list of six books below:

SIX GREAT BOOKS FOR MANAGERS

1. *The Go-Giver* by Bob Burg and John David Mann
2. *First, Break all the Rules* by Marcus Buckingham and Curt Coffman
3. *Gung-Ho* by Ken Blanchard and Sheldon Bowles
4. *Raving Fans: A Revolutionary Approach to Customer Service* by Ken Blanchard and Sheldon Bowles
5. *The One-Minute Manager* by Ken Blanchard and Spencer Johnson
6. *The Seven Habits of Highly Effective People* by Stephen R. Covey

Each manager was given an opportunity and challenge: Over the course of six months, take 30 days to read each book. Within seven days, turn in a three-question book report. If the report is turned in by the seventh day of the month after it has been read, receive a $50 cash bonus for each book. That's an opportunity for $300 in cash! But wait, there's more ...

If all six book reports are turned in on a timely basis, the manager is awarded an iPad. Every single manager who has gone through this program has earned the iPad. It's a huge incentive! What do we get out of it? We get everybody talking the same exact language. Everyone is on the same page. I can walk into a restaurant and say, "I think Justina might need a one-minute feedback. She just did xyz." The manager says, "Great, I noticed that too. Boom-boom-boom." Just like that. Getting everybody on the same page, speaking the same language, has been a wonderful benefit.

Format has been a remarkably valuable tool to train the managers who train the associates, which puts us in the position to manage managers. Smart. Not only did we move from serving every guest and managing every associate, now we manage our managers, who are accountable to manage associates. Beyond that, we've grown to the point where we've developed regional management. For each elevation in this process, we elevate too. We are now at the point

> We are now at the point where we manage systems and regional managers, who manage the general managers, who manage the associates, who take care of our guests in the most loving way.

where we manage systems and regional managers, who manage the general managers, who manage the associates, who take care of our guests in the most loving way.

REPLICATING YOURSELF
THROUGH YOUR PEOPLE

Dan Kennedy says, "Stop doing 'the one thing' over and over and over. Figure out how to do it once and make it replicable." While we can teach guest service, one thing we realize we can't teach is personality. Instead, we hire for personality, for a set of measurable attributes through a systemic approach. Our president, Shila Morris, developed a Superstar Hiring process. Using our ideal associates as a model, Shila created a profile of what we love about the way they serve and behave, and we now measure prospective associates against this profile. We have legendary marketing and business guru Bill Glazer to thank for the idea and the example. We look for people who can smile, interact, and make eye contact. While we can't mandate personality, we absolutely, positively, can mandate behavior,

> While we can't mandate personality, we absolutely, positively, can mandate behavior, and we do.

and we do. We're able to do that through our comprehensive hiring and training system. We've laid out our expectations and hold associates accountable to them.

As Blanchard and Ridge said in *Helping People Win at Work,* "Employees want to be happy at work." Training with built-in accountability is a major key to this success.

TRAINING WITHOUT WIGGLE ROOM

I recently walked into one of our restaurants and said to the manager, "Oh, I see you have some new associates!" This was after all these intensive, accountable programs had been implemented. I said, "Have they all gone through the training?"

"Yes, they've all signed off," she answered.

"Great!" I walked up to one of the new associates and said, "Hi, I'm Misty Young. I'm one of the owners."

She replied, "Hi, Misty. I recognized you. I'm so glad to meet you" and told me her name.

"Have you gone through all the training materials?" I asked, and since she answered in the affirmative, I continued, "Great. I'm going to give you a quick quiz. "Tell me the seven steps of the host mantra."

Well, she was flustered, telling me, "Greet, you know, um, seat, um ..."

She looked around, and her eyes were kind of flitting, and I said, "You have not actually finished this training material, have you?"

Her answer was simply, "Well, um, my computer broke and ... and I ..."

I looked at her and said, "Your manager says you signed off. You just told me that you went through the training. You lied."

You can imagine how disappointed and angry I was. After assuring and refining our solid training process and creating all this great material, I was very disappointed in her. I continued, "I cannot believe you just told me you did this training and you obviously didn't."

She shrugged her shoulders and scrunched up her face and questioned, "I'm sorry?"

No, "I'm sorry" didn't fly. She was off that floor and off our payroll that very day. Here's why I chose her for the pop quiz in the first place: I saw her wipe a table with the bar towel, and then wipe the seat of the chair with the same bar towel, and then wipe the table again with the same bar towel. Ewwwww!

You don't wipe a table and the seat of a chair with the same bar cloth in my restaurant. Ever. You just don't do that. It's gross, it's disgusting, it's unsanitary.

There are few things in life I abhor. Incompetence and lying top the list. And, for those wondering, "Well, what is that host mantra anyway?" Here it is, a seven-step process: greet, seat, beverage, bus, take payment, clean, start over! How hard is that?

Excellent, accountable, measurable training is how we replicate ourselves through our associates. There can be no wiggle room if you want to succeed.

We've already established there are only two kinds of people in your restaurant: guests and associates. You have to treat each of them with the ultimate respect, and your associates must be your partners in treating guests with the ultimate respect. There's no wiggle room there either.

There can be no wiggle room if you want to succeed.

Your associates cannot roll eyes. They cannot flub on specials. They can't touch the business end of silverware. They can't wrap their hands over a coffee cup rim or hold a wine glass at the lip. They've got to wash their hands frequently and maintain a clean restaurant. These are basic expectations to maintain, and whatever the expectations are in your restaurant, it's completely a reflection of you personally, *and so are your associates*. They're not mind readers; it's your job to develop strategic, accountable training materials to help them be happy at work and help everyone mutually achieve their goals.

There must be no wiggle room in how your associates treat your restaurant's most important asset: your guests. Yes, you've got a cool restaurant and great menu. But if you've got associates not doing it your way precisely, you might as well shut the doors. You're going to end up out of business sooner or later.

VIDEO TRAINING IS EASY

When you create something like a video training program, you can be precise and it doesn't have to be difficult or expensive. You can use your iPhone. Seriously, make a one minute training video with your iPhone. "Here's how I want you to set the table." Boom, bam, done. One minute. Post it in a private link on YouTube, have your people watch and sign off that they did so. Check the checker who checks the checker! Be sure they did it! Place sign-offs in a personnel folder. Remember: Find the things you do over and over and stop wasting your time. Do it one more time for the camera and be done with it. One and done.

Yes, we created scripts. Yes, we hired a professional videographer. It doesn't have to be hard. None of the stuff we're talking about in this book has to be complicated; *you just have to do it.*

Be accountable! Our first set of videos was completely unscripted, literally. We had the topics and did a point and shoot with minor editing. They sufficed, but as the company grew in sophistication, and as our leadership began to shift and emerge, the need to update our videos was clear. President Shila created an entire new expanded set of scripted videos. Our associates love them, and we've shared them as an example with many clients and colleagues throughout the industry.

We grow in many ways as we replicate ourselves through our associates. Love of our businesses, families, and ourselves transfers to associates and guests. *That's a recipe for success.* Well-trained associates have a better opportunity of intentionally delivering a great experience along with consistency and courtesy. No matter who is serving the guests, their experience will always be of the same high quality.

IT'S LIKE MAGIC: HAPPY ASSOCIATES ATTRACT HAPPY GUESTS

People want to be happy at work. They don't want to come to work and be bummed out. They don't want to come to work and feel badgered and beleaguered. They want to do a good job. They want to know the culture, the rules, and the expectations. Your goal as the restaurant owner is to give associates every single tool you can to help them be happy.

How fun is it to go to work and be recognized publicly? It's fun! Our associates often find special call-outs from guest surveys, listing them by name with the details of the great service they delivered. Our managers use colored markers to highlight great guest comments and post them throughout the restaurant for everyone to see. How cool is that?

It might be as simple as a pat on the back, or, going back to the days when your kids were little, a star chart on the wall recognizing associates for having done something great. In our restaurants we also do small things as easy as publicly handing out candy bars and compliments in regular meetings.

It might be as simple as creating a Sunday $20 bill incentive. We'll post $20 and say, "Okay, the first person who sells a pitcher of mimosa gets to hold this $20 until the next person sells a pitcher."

Throughout the day, the $20 bill floats from person to person, hand to hand, and ends up in the pocket of the person who sold *the most pitchers* of mimosa for the day. Now, you can do the math: a pitcher of mimosa is $21.99, (about five mimosas, which normally run $4.99 each). The $20 is a huge incentive for our associates. It makes them happy and they get to make the guest happy with the special discount. The incentive rewards the associate for what they're doing every day, which is to help the guest have a great experience. Is it fun to go to a restaurant and get a little mimosa buzz? Oh heck, yes, it is.

What do you want your happy associates to do? To give your guests the best experience possible. That means giving them all the options available from mimosas and Bloody Marys to upgrades and add-ons. Making suggestions is not an evil selling technique. It's an opportunity for the guest to have the best experience possible. Would you like to add melted cheese and grilled onions to your spuds? These inter-actions and suggestions are simple and of help to the guest, while adding to your own bottom line. As an added incentive to your associates, their work often increases the bill the guest is calculating the tip on. Everyone benefits from this.

Here's a weird thing: Never once was I offered a mimosa as a guest at the original Squeeze. They were so buried on the menu, I didn't even know they were there. My all-time drink of choice? Champagne. Add orange juice to make it a healthy (ahem, vitamin C) breakfast choice? Well, yeah! If you come to the Squeeze today, you can't miss the mimosas. We'll be sure to suggest one.

We see the importance of the well-trained, happy associate in the triangle system. Next, we'll take an in-depth look at guest experience management, the actual how to make your guests happy.

INGREDIENTS FOR SUCCESS

1. Think "we" first. Solo is old school; social is new school.
2. Say "Thank you" to your associates today. Find five ways to praise and thank them and then do it without hesitation. It's magical.
3. Write a mission statement. It doesn't have to be perfect on first draft. Copy mine if you want.
4. Check the checker who checks the checker.
5. Make a list of your top-five most common training tasks. Write them out in perfect detail from step one to finish. Bam. That's the start of your training system.
6. Check your bus trays and trashcans to see what's being wasted.

7. Buy and read a book; start with *The Go-Giver.*

8. Assign books to your associates and incentivize their reading.

9. Replicate yourself. Leave no wiggle room.

10. Help your associates be happy. Start by being happy yourself. It's attractive.

CHAPTER EIGHT

Do the Right Thing: Serve Rock Stars Every Day

You can have the coolest restaurant and best associates in the world, great training, critically acclaimed food, highest, most amazing standards of cleanliness, but if you don't have any guests, you don't have a business. The guest is the most valuable asset in the restaurant business, and must be treated as such.

Of course you already know that. Your main question in this chapter is, "How do I get more guests in my restaurant?" The answer: Treat them like rock stars. They've got to have a great experience and you've got to stay in communication with them.

Whatever the vibe of your restaurant, stay true to the vibe if it's successful, and make it work for the guests. Do that by emphasizing your guests as the center of everyone's focus.

We'll also discuss a no-brainer business building strategy a bit later in this chapter.

It doesn't mean your restaurant has to be like the Squeeze In with a fun, high-energy vibe. That's our style, though maybe not yours, which may be high-end, fine dining, red velvet, dark curtains, or romance with candlelight and tiny tables. Whatever the vibe of your restaurant, stay true to the vibe if it's successful, and make it work for the guests. Do that by emphasizing your guests as the center of everyone's focus.

Restaurant Success Star

Beyond all the other things, the guest's experience matters most. Yes, the food matters, the service and cleanliness matter; that's all part of the overall experience. Once you've trained your associates, and they know exactly what you expect of them, *you can hold them (and yourself) account-*

able to it. Only then can you provide a consistently great experience to your guests.

GEM: GUEST EXPERIENCE MANAGEMENT

At the Squeeze, we focus on GEM (Guest Experience Management). We discuss GEM with our associates regularly. On Saturdays and Sundays, an associate is often assigned a floating GEM position throughout the restaurant.

I'll walk into a Squeeze on a busy weekend and check the associate assignment board. Some associates are obviously serving, some are hosting, some are "GEMing."

GEM means the associate is not only assuring the guests are having an exceptional experience but *other associates are too*. We feel it's really important to encourage associate-to-associate service. In fact, we get e-mails and survey comments like this all the time: "I couldn't believe it. It seemed like I didn't have a server, I had all servers. Everyone helped me!"

I had a guest ask me, "Come on, (he's winking and nodding), you've got shock collars or something, right? Everyone's so happy here. How did you do that? No, really, how did you do that?"

I just said, "We've got a comprehensive training program. We value our associates and have very clear guest service expectations. We hold them accountable, we ask them to have fun, and we ask them to treat you with the utmost respect and courtesy, realizing and knowing that you are the

most important and most valuable asset this company has."
He smiled and said, "I still think it's shock collars!"

GREAT SERVICE IS GREAT VALUE

When guests know they're getting their money's worth, it makes them happy. We're not a cheap place to eat, *and we're in a town with a lot of cheap places to eat.* We have a $22 omelette on the menu. That's a mark of business success. If you do things the right way, you don't have to compete on price, and good guests know this. That's not to say we don't offer specials and promotions; we surely do, but we do it through our rock-solid EggHead Breakfast Club—and for members only!

A VALUES BASED COMPANY

We're a values-based company. This paragraph from our code of business conduct precedes our values. It reads: "We understand the importance of follow up, of a learning environment, a clear vision and rank-ordered values. Our values help keep our tribe focused on serving *each other and guests* every day."

These are the rank-ordered Squeeze In values:

1. Do the right thing.
2. Serve guests and each other with respect and courtesy in a safe, healthy environment.

3. Daily improvement. Make it better every day.
4. Understand the value of tribe success through individual success.
5. Own it and passionately act on it.
6. Sustainably support the Squeeze In economy, which in turn supports us all.

We believe our associates know what doing the right thing means in their gut. They know it; they get it. If an associate sees a colleague serving a guest poorly, making an inappropriate comment, or doing something unsafe, they know in their gut what the right thing to do is. We trust our associates. Our values are rank ordered in case a situation arises when the answer isn't completely clear. There are always gray areas. In all cases, the number-one, rank-ordered value to fall back on is: *do the right thing*. Remember, we built our code of business conduct from the great book *Helping People Win at Work* by Ken Blanchard and Garry Ridge. I encourage you to read it. Our code of business conduct is available via my website, as is my full and constantly growing recommended reading list.

SERVING KINDNESS

We serve guests, and we do it in a way that helps us also serve each other. We encourage our associates to ask each other throughout the day, "Is there anything I can do for you?" How many restaurants can you walk into where the front of the house is serving the kitchen in the middle of the mayhem on a weekend morning? You'll see that at the Squeeze.

The front-of-house staff walk right into the kitchen. "Guys, you're doing such a great job; you're working so hard. Who needs some coffee or orange juice?" We encourage them to serve each other because the Squeeze In is a full representation of each of the owners: Shila, Chad, Gary, and Misty. Each of us is represented in this business. Each of us strives to be of service to others and encourages them to do the same. Even as a family, we strive to serve each other.

My personal mantras are "Thank you" and "How may I serve you?" I ask my associates to also ask, "How may I serve you" and ask each other "How do we, together, best serve our guests?" I believe serving is a noble and kind task we can provide each other, no matter who we are or what our station in life. To do it with intention? Priceless.

KNOW YOUR TARGET

We are absolutely at the high end of the breakfast restaurants in our region. Someone has to be at the top of the price chain and I don't mind it being us. There are many competitors out there in cheap breakfast. That's not our brand.

We pay well. We offer and cover 75 percent of the health insurance premiums for eligible associates. And guess what? We've been doing that since 2009, long before it was mandated.

Why? Because it is the right thing to do, and because our business is a high-end business (even if it is fun and funky!), and our guests value that. Our value is cemented in a great experience: fabulous food served by genuinely friendly, well-trained people in a healthy, safe, clean, fun environment. Our $21.99 Holy Crab! omelette features a full quarter-pound of king crab sautéed in butter with green onions, folded in with Monterey jack cheese, topped with avocado and lemon slices. It's freaking outrageous.

Guess what? We sell a lot of Holy Crab! omelettes. Why? Because it's a fantastic product for one thing, and because we have established ourselves as a premium brand guests value doing business with.

Reno, where most of our locations exist, is casino country. Other places offer ham and eggs for $2.99, steak and eggs for $4.99. We don't compete with that. That's someone else's market segment. We own a different market segment: service, quality, and experience dining, a position we much prefer.

Every once in a while someone will say, "These prices are outrageous." We had a guy visit our second location in Reno at nearly closing time on a midweek day, soon after we had our grand opening. Only a couple of guests were there at 1:50 p.m. (we close at 2:00 p.m.) when this guy walked in. The lunch crowd had already gone back to work.

He sat down, took a look at the menu, chucked it on the table, looked around and said, "No wonder this place is empty.

These prices are outrageous. You guys won't last a month in this town," and with that, he got up and walked out.

He crushed everyone working that day, especially Chad, who would have been his server. It was hard to hear, but guess what? Not only have we surpassed his surly prediction of "not lasting a month" in that location, we've more than doubled our business footprint (and raised our prices) in that time, adding two additional Reno area locations. That one guy is not our target. There are a whole lot more people who are ready to walk in and put down good money for great service and excellent food in a clean, safe, healthy environment with genuinely friendly associates. That's why our guests keep coming back. That and, as Amanda said, because we love them!

WHEN THINGS GO AWRY

Sometimes things just go wrong. It happens. Omelettes get mixed up, side orders get forgotten, food takes too long, the salad slides onto the guest's lap. Whatever happens, we address problems with kindness and courtesy. We have a saying, "The guest isn't always right, but the guest is always the guest." When you're a guest in our house, you'll be treated with the utmost respect. We created and train our associates to use the LATTE approach to guest service issues.

> "The guest isn't always right, but the guest is always the guest."

Here's a section from our manager training guide:

Guest Problems: The LATTE Approach

We believe mistakes are opportunities to learn—they are inevitable but not fatal. We strive to reduce the number of mistakes made in the day-to-day operation of our restaurants, living the value, "Daily improvement—making it better every day." We learn from mistakes and evolve.

- listen
- apologize (acknowledgize)
- take action
- thank
- evolve

Managers lead the tribe through any and all problems and do whatever it takes to assure guest satisfaction, whether comping a beverage, all beverages, an entrée or an entire ticket, whatever it takes. Your goal is to resolve the situation satisfactorily for the guest. The worst thing we can do is to send an unhappy guest out our door. Use your judgment and keep our number-one value in mind: *Do the right thing*.

Download a printable LATTE card over at my website.

We all know things go awry. What sets us apart is we've got strategies and tactics to deal with it. In addition to any in house response, an e-mail complaint usually gets a personal reply from President Shila and sometimes a handwritten card through the mail as well. We may add points to the guest's EggHead account to generate an automatic gift certificate. Sometimes all it takes to make it right is to acknowledge and thank the guest, and in all cases, we use the problem as an opportunity to improve, evolve.

> Tell them what you expect, how you want everything handled, and then hold yourself and your associates accountable to the standard by monitoring and managing your system.

You can do this in your restaurant too, but you've got to remember your associates aren't mind readers. Tell them what you expect, how you want everything handled, and then hold yourself and your associates accountable to the standard by monitoring and managing your system. It works for everyone and will give your guests the best possible experience. You know what else? It will help you sleep better at night.

NO RISK: GIVE YOUR GUESTS A GUARANTEE

Successful restaurateurs do whatever it takes to assure an excellent guest experience, right? If the guest hates the meal, it will be replaced. If the experience is terrible, you're going to make good on it. Since you already guarantee your products and service in this way, why not take all the mystery out of it by offering an outrageous guarantee? Not only should you offer it, you should promote it in every way possible. *Take all the risk out for the guest.* The Squeeze's outrageous guarantee is: "You'll love our food or it's free."

I don't like giving food away, so, through our attention to detail and our commitment to a great guest experience, our goal is to make it right no matter what. Our guarantee can be found on our menu, website, and even on our business cards. There's no mystery here. We strive to do it right and we make good on our promise. Even though we widely promote our outrageous guarantee in as many ways as we can, it's a rare occurrence for a guest to make a claim on it. We stand by our products and services and guests don't take unfair advantage of it.

WHEN GUESTS LOVE YOU BACK

I recently received an e-mail from an independent restaurateur. She said, "We've been checking out your website. We love your menu and everything. We want to open a second location, and we're hitting a wall securing funding. We have some personal savings, could do another place on a shoestring, but I want to do it right. I need more money. Would you mind sharing how you've managed to fund opening two new restaurants in 16 months?"

In 2008, when we opened our second location in Reno, we had never built a restaurant before. We used our best judgment moving forward and felt certain we could capture the essence of what was so cool about our little tiny restaurant in the mountains, the original "mother-ship" location in Truckee. We were so excited to get this second place up and running. We felt that we had captured the vibe and the atmosphere and the ambiance of it. Here's how we knew we had met our goal.

A lovely couple had moved to Reno from the Midwest. Since they were new in town, they asked their real estate agent, "Hey, where's a good place to have breakfast?" Without hesitation, their agent said, "You've got to go to the Squeeze In." To open a brand-new restaurant 30 miles away in a brand-new town, and real estate agents are already talking about you? *That's cool.*

These folks came into the restaurant, and it just so happens this was at the time when we owners were still on the floor, serving guests. My business partner Chad served this couple and blew them away with our signature service, which is attentive, courteous, kind, genuine, and meaningful. Then, the food was outrageous, fresh, and served with love.

I can't emphasize enough everything we do every day— we receive, we prep, slice, dice, chop, clean, wash, cook, serve—all our actions start *with love.* Every action is intentionally surrounded with love; it really is the secret recipe. If associates fall out of love, we lovingly promote them to guests if we can't help them find their heart again. That's not to say we never just straight up fire people. Theft? Lying? No call, no show? You're gone. You're done. No wiggle room.

We knew we captured the Squeeze essence because this couple has told us their story several times over the years. After they had this outrageous experience with Chad, they said, "Oh my gosh, we could not believe the level of service we had from this young man. It had to be a fluke. That could not possibly happen again. Let's go back tomorrow and try."

They came back the next day. Chad wasn't there. They told us they were let down, bummed out. Thought it might have sucked, it didn't suck. The server was amazing—kind, courteous, compassionate, genuine, helpful, fast. The food was fresh and tasty. We see these wonderful guests regularly at the Squeeze, and they have become great personal friends as well all these years later.

These guests come to our private events, to our baby showers, graduations, birthday and anniversary parties, to our pumpkin carving events. We go out together as couples. Whatever we do, these great folks are invited. They appreciate us and we appreciate them. This is part of how we have created a great guest experience.

We make our guests feel special because we don't treat them as a transaction. We think about and focus on building a lifetime relationship with our guests.

> We make our guests feel special because we don't treat them as a transaction.

Millions of people go out to eat every single day. *Guests prefer dining where they are appreciated and honored.*

SO, WHERE'D WE GET THE MONEY?

This brings me back to answering the woman's e-mail about getting funding for her restaurant. What I'm going to tell you blows away everyone I tell this story to, and it also lets you know how truly loyal our guests are to us, and how much we are valued in our communities.

I told the woman who e-mailed, "We crowd-sourced, essentially, to raise the money. We have 52,751 individuals (at that time) in our database. Do you have a database?" She didn't.

Dan Kennedy says, "If you aren't making lists, you probably aren't making a lot of money either. If you don't have a list, you don't have a business."

If you don't have a database, you're at a serious disadvantage as a business. Independent restaurants are not only competing with each other, but today's dining-out dollar is shared among chains, grocery stores, fast food outlets, frozen delivery services, personal chefs, food trucks, and even food ordered online. Independents need every edge they can get, which is one of the reasons we love our EggHead Breakfast Club so much (more at MistyYoung.com). The EggHead Club has automated our marketing and done miracles for our business.

To grow our company, we mailed letters to a very select group of guests from our database. Our selection criteria were based on visit frequency, spending history, geographic region, and longevity. We mailed out a great offer of full-value gift cards purchased at a substantial discount, coupled with outrageous loyalty club bonuses (free food, VIP parties, T-shirts, bags of coffee, fruit bowls, mimosas, and more) and brought in over $75,000 *in cash*. This was huge for us. The economy wasn't rebounding; credit was tight. We didn't have any lines of credit. The outreach to the guests in our club, our own house list, was the kicker.

The offers and bonuses were substantial for our guests, who were stoked to receive them, and we were stoked to put $75,000 in the bank and open new restaurants. We'll have a different growth model soon.

By the end of this year, we'll grow the Squeeze In by allowing independents directly into our family as we've launched a national licensing process. We like to think of ourselves as a "famchise" in that we'll be incredibly selective whom we'll allow into the Squeeze In family. After all, our brand, our systems, our nearly a decade of work to build our reputation is on the line, as are our relationships and reliability. We know exactly what it takes for long-term success and will only accept the most qualified partners. We're excited. You can find details at both SqueezeIn.com and on MistyYoung.com.

LOYALTY PROGRAMS WORK

If I haven't hammered on it enough yet: if you don't have a database marketing loyalty program, you're in a bad way. Really and truly, go spend a bit of time to watch the webinar that Rory and I put together. I've negotiated well for my clients. Rory offers a Free $5,000 Marketing Jump Start (you do pay a small fully refundable deposit.) All you do is sign up members and Rory's team does their entire marketing program for your restaurant *for Free for 90 days. Go right to the webinar from my website MistyYoung.com.*

Free postcards, free printing, free postage, free e-mails, free surveys—they pay for everything for the first 90 days. *I counsel every client to get the most out of that 90 days. Sign up as many people as you can and get all the marketing you can for free.* Yes, after the 90 days, you do pay for campaigns you run. You decide what campaigns you want to execute, what offers you'd like to make, whom you'd like to target, how much money you'd like to earn all the while charting your ROI through an intuitive and detailed graphical user interface.

It's a seriously sophisticated, comprehensive, flexible program but very easy to use, designed for independents like us. I cannot possibly be more adamant about the Squeeze's success and growth stemming from our strategic use of this program. Yes, sophisticated

---

The days of rinky-dink marketing are over. Sophistication and options rule.

---

marketing is key. Yes, social media is too. Having your guests opt in, well, that's just plain smart. Your guests should be locked in to your iron-clad marketing system. If you don't do it, some other restaurant surely will. The days of rinky-dink marketing are over. Sophistication and options rule.

I'd be happy to share the letters that helped us raise $75,000. They are available at MistyYoung.com.

The competition is growing more fierce every day and it goes beyond other restaurants. Grocery stores with premade foods served buffet style, those frozen dinners in a box delivered to your door—everyone is moving into the food business. There's a lot of competition. You need a sharp edge.

DEVELOP A REFERRAL CULTURE

At the beginning of the chapter, I promised a strategy to bring in more guests. Happy guests want to tell others about their experience at your restaurant. The single most effective way to build your business (and by far the least expensive) is to develop a referral culture. It's only a three-letter word: ask. Ask your happy guests to introduce your restaurant to their friends, colleagues, and family members. The stronger your relationship with your guests, the more likely they are to continue to support your business and bring their friends. Ask them to help you build your business and ultimately serve your community. They'll love to do it for you. I have a white paper on the website about developing a referral culture. Stop by and pick it up.

THE POWER AND IMPORTANCE OF "THANK YOU"

Do your associates regularly thank guests for visiting your restaurant? As we've discussed, the guest is the single most valuable asset of your restaurant. No guest, no business. We encourage learning guest names and as often as possible, genuinely expressing our thanks to our guests. We strive for every guest to hear "Thank you" on every single visit. It's important.

I personally take it a step further and use several tools to thank guests. I'm not in the restaurants any more to do it in person, so I send cards. I've used two methods: I designed and had professionally printed my own Squeeze In thank-you cards and keep a ready supply and postage on hand (see sample on the website). I regularly review the EggHead Breakfast Club database and mail completely personal, handwritten thank-you cards to selected guests. Most times these are literally just a thank-you card with a note, something to the effect of, "Hi Mark and Candy! Thank you for being our guests. We know you have many choices and we're thankful you choose the Squeeze. With love, Misty and Gary." The personal card is mailed in a hand-addressed envelope, with a real, live stamp. I get thank-you cards in the mail and Facebook shout-outs for thank-you cards I've sent! I usually send 50–75 handwritten cards monthly (pictures on the website).

Young & Morris Families
Squeeze In
5020 Las Brisas Blvd., A5
Reno NV 89523

Misty Young
The Restaurant Lady
97913 Holly Lane
Brookings OR 97415

© SendOutCards
www.SendOutCards.com/MistyYoung

2_panel (uv)
151991-162692

This card is printed on recycled paper

Young Family --

Thank you for helping us live our dream. We love
serving you, and our communities and being a
local, family owned business. Thank you for
being such an important part of our continued
success.

With great appreciation,

Shila and Chad Morris
Gary and Misty Young

With the exponential growth of our guest list, I've recently begun using a very cool tool, SendOutCards, which has helped me still be personal but automated. I can upload a list from my in-house database and send out personalized, beautiful, custom cards to hundreds of people at the press of a button. SendOutCards has been a true time saver. I love the company and the product so much I became an agent for them, now sharing the product and service with other businesses and individuals. SendOutCards can help you deepen your guest relationships. See a case study at the website or head over to www.SendOutCards.com/MistyYoung to try the system free and mail a completely custom card on me. Send a beautiful card to someone you love!

THE BOTTOM LINE

When you love your guests, they keep coming back. When you communicate with and reward them, they love you even more. When you focus on guest experience management and make every guest know they are a gem to you, you seal the deal.

INGREDIENTS FOR SUCCESS

1. Download the Restaurant Success Star at the website. Post it in the associate area of your restaurant.

2. Establish your own GEM approach in your restaurant.

3. Become a values-based company. Share to get your associates on board.

4. Give and expect kindness and courtesy.

5. Know your target. Figure it out by looking at your current guests.

6. Implement the LATTE approach. It works in all restaurants, not just breakfast.

7. Create an outrageous guarantee. Tell everyone, everywhere you can.

8. Go sign up for the Free $5,000 Marketing Jump Start trial (yes, I keep saying this one!). Find the link on my website, MistyYoung.com

9. Ask for referrals and say "Thank you" in as many ways as you can. (Go make a free card through SendOutCards on me!)

CHAPTER NINE

Modern Marketing: You Do the Math, Be Social!

Law #5, the law of marketing: the business must use multimedia tools to communicate on a timely basis with guests and associates in relevant, meaningful ways.

My marketing mentor and business coach, Rory Fatt, says, "Marketing is math." He teaches his coaching clients to get their emotions out of the way, allowing results to speak for themselves. He introduced me to measurable marketing, some tactics were beautiful and elegant and some, I thought, were quirky or cheesy and probably wouldn't work but did wonders. He taught me how to prepare, deliver, and measure the effects of my marketing efforts, and then built the database system we now use to power the EggHead Breakfast Club. I'm thrilled to have gotten to know Rory over the years. I appreciate his marketing-is-math metaphor.

In his book, *Restaurant Marketing in the New Economy,* Rory says, "The most successful restaurant owners don't look at marketing as a cost but, rather, as an investment. The one thing that's irrefutable is the restaurants that are spending the most on marketing, as a percentage of sales, actually have the highest profit." I have followed Rory Fatt, Dan Kennedy, and Bill Glazer's counsel now for years. Lest you think that makes me a one-trick pony, consider I'm riding a winning horse. I'll mail you Rory's excellent soft-cover book for free (while supplies last), available at my website.

As restaurateurs and marketers, we've learned we have to work on our business instead of exclusively in it if we want to elevate over time. We've got to create a lean, mean, service machine to take excellent care of our guests, and we've got to communicate with them. We've got to cut the fat from our businesses, especially our marketing. Independent restaurateurs cannot depend on old-school broadcasting or nontargeted marketing tactics. We have to be mathematicians in our approach.

YOU CAN DO THE MATH

I'm talking basic math, not calculus or trigonometry! It's true I *failed* every math class I ever took till I got to college, but I had to pass math to graduate and I was motivated. My first semester, the math professor offered extra credit for reading. I knew I'd need it, so I picked *Overcoming Math Anxiety*

> Independent restaurateurs cannot depend on old-school broadcasting or nontargeted marketing tactics.

by Sheila Tobias from the list. Best. Decision. Ever. I literally read that little book and my math avoidance and anxiety shifted in the moment. I got As in every single college math class afterward, including probability and statistics.

The math we do in day-to-day business isn't difficult, just the basics: addition, subtraction, multiplication, and division. It may look like algebra with equations such as $x + y = z/n$ and many variables can be substituted, but it's still basic. You'll want to get used to figuring out your marketing investment, how many pieces you send (deliver, pass out, whatever) how much postage is involved, and how many resulted in sales, and use all of that along with your cost of goods sold to determine your return on investment or ROI. If you'd like, there's an ROI calculator spreadsheet download over at the website.

Of course, for us, all of this is done automatically by campaigns we do through the program. We also do some marketing independently. Not everything goes through the database, so we've got to know how to calculate.

MAKE SOCIAL MEDIA WORK FOR YOU

Law #5, the law of marketing, clearly states the business must use multimedia tools to communicate in a timely manner with guests and associates in relevant, meaningful ways. Our effort cannot be stagnant or single channel. We've got to broaden our reach and depth to be relevant and meaningful.

Remember, there are three types of media: owned, earned, and paid. You decide how to use all of it. Very simply, you must have social media in your toolkit; it isn't going away. In fact, it's growing rapidly.

On Facebook, if you search "restaurant," unsurprisingly, you'll find all the major players there. Remember, the chains are successful not because they have systems, but because they use systems every day. Social media must be successfully integrated into your marketing system. If you don't have a system, wouldn't now be a good time to build one? Yes! I've got a marketing plan download for your use over at MistyYoung.com.

If you search on Facebook for your mom-and-pop competitors from down the street, you probably won't find them, and that's partly why your restaurant must be there. You've got to meet your guests where they are. Currently, 50 percent of independent restaurants don't even have a website. Um, *hello?* Where is your guest? *On the Internet!*

They're on their phones, laptops, desktop computers, and tablets. They're in their cars using GPS systems (powered by Google), deciding where they're going to eat. They're on chain restaurant's mobile websites. Do you have a website? More importantly, do you have a mobile website? Here's how to see the distinct difference between the two: visit www.

squeezein.com from your laptop or desktop and then visit the same website from your mobile device and see what happens, automatically.

Guests, and potential guests are looking for you, in what they may feel is a game of hide and seek. *Don't hide!* Be visible and appear in search results when they're looking. Social media is a great way to level the playing field, and, for the most part, it's free.

In her book *How to Become a Social Media Ninja, New York Times* social media blogger Melinda Emerson says, "Larger companies with big advertising budgets no longer have the upper hand in business." In this power-packed book, Melinda suggests using the help

> Social media is a great way to level the playing field, and, for the most part, it's free.

mantra in connecting with audiences: help others; engage people; listen first; promote yourself with care. One of her Black Belt Tips is: "Invest in a branded Facebook fan page and timeline graphic. Allow your fans to write on your wall and be quick to respond to any posts from fans."

Ultimately, pick a social forum and get good at it, keeping in mind you've got to learn to walk before you can run. Are you a chef? Would cooking demonstrations of your signature menu items be valuable, interesting YouTube content for your guests? Do you have a fabulous well-known drink in your bar? Could you post recipes? Cooking tips? Tweets about trends? The possibilities are endless, and, some might say, overwhelming. It's the Wild West right now, all over again, a continuously emerging interactive (aka social) frontier. Pick a platform, get good at it, and expand from there. You don't have to be all things to all people; you just have to be relevant to your guests and locatable in the social space.

At the Squeeze we do everything we possibly can to keep up with new digital tools. According to YouTube's press page, *72 hours of video is uploaded to YouTube every minute.* And that number is increasing, exponentially. We are making sure to regularly publish Squeeze content to YouTube. Are you doing the same for your restaurant?

Here are more outrageous stats: *4 billion hours of YouTube videos are watched monthly.* And again, that number is increasing daily. In fact, YouTube states traffic from mobile devices tripled in 2011. Wow. YouTube is the number-two search engine in the world, second only to Google.

While mind boggling, these statistics affirm yet again that for independent restaurateurs, we must be where our guests are: in the social theater.

While we as restaurateurs think about our restaurants 24/7, guests don't just immediately and automatically think about our restaurants. We talked about guest experience management and about meeting guest expectations. When the guest is asking their prime question, "What does success look like to me?" when they're thinking about their birthday breakfast or celebrating their team's big win, your restaurant needs to pop into their mind. How do you make that happen? You have to plan for it (there's that four letter word again)!

You make it happen by being where your guest is. Your guest is on Twitter, on YouTube, on Facebook, FourSquare, Pinterest, and Instagram to mention just a few. Your restaurant must be there too, with interactive, relevant, interesting content, videos, photos, recipes, tips—you name it.

Here are Misty's three Rs of branding success:

1. Reputation: build it, monitor and maintain it with vigilance;
2. Relationship: the basis for everything you do in business;
3. Reliability: if you're not reliable and consistent, you're out of business;

Your guest is relying on finding you in the social space. Be reliable.

SOCIAL MEDIA IS INTERACTIVE

It's not about selling, selling, selling. In fact if you're on Facebook saying, "Our special is this," "Our special is that," "Our appetizer is this," "Our soup of the day is that," you are BORING. Big capital letters, B-O-R-I-N-G. People will tune out.

It's called social media for a reason: it's two-way, multiway. It's interactive. It's not old-school broadcast. It's new-school narrowcast, even microcast. It's individual, conversational, social. Listening and responding, posting comments and asking questions. Engaging, interactive, part of a conversation. Two-way, or many-way! Remember, solo is old school, social is new school. Build relationships.

> It's called social media for a reason: it's two-way, multiway. It's interactive. It's not old-school broadcast. It's new-school narrowcast, even microcast. It's individual, conversational, social. Listening and responding, posting comments and asking questions. Engaging, interactive, part of a conversation. Two-way, or many-way! Remember, solo is old school, social is new school. Build relationships.

I spoke with someone recently who said, "I don't get Twitter. I tried it. It's not valuable. I post and post and post, and I never get anything back." I said, "Well, do you ever respond to other people's posts?"

"No, why would I?"

I could hardly respond. Well, that's what you have to do. You've got to be listening to what people are saying and responding, commenting, sharing, being relevant.

For instance, yesterday somebody tweeted a picture and comment about an omelette they had enjoyed at the Squeeze. We immediately tweeted back to this guest, "Thank you so much for posting; that's really cool, thank you." It's just a thank-you, but it let him know we were paying attention and knew he had enjoyed the Squeeze In. It became a conversation. It validates what he tweeted. Of course, we retweeted his tweet to our own stream. Our conversation then became part of the larger conversation among the couple of thousand people tuned into his and our tweets.

Let's say you go to a cocktail party. That's a social event, right? Who's the most engaging person at the party? *Hint: they're listening.*

On listening, John Maxwell says, "What most people really want is to be listened to, respected, and understood." We can all do that with a little effort.

The best conversationalists aren't talking *to* you; they're listening to you. The best conversationalists say, "Tell me about your business, your grandchildren, your kids in school. Tell me about your passion." They are actively listening, hearing, responding relevantly, and being interested, not ramping up their brain with what to say next. The same is true in the social space.

At the end of the party you say to yourself, "Wow, wasn't Kim amazing? What a great conversationalist!" What do you know about Kim? Probably very little. What does Kim know about you? Likely a great deal because Kim was actively engaging with you. And Kim is obviously smart and will likely engage at an even deeper level on the next opportunity because she *listened.*

That's what you have to do in social media. You have to be social. You have to "party with a purpose." Your purpose is to listen, engage, interact, be relevant, be interested. Then every once in a while you throw something out there that says, "Our special this week is blah-blah." "Our soup of the day is," and so on. "We're offering an exclusive bonus on our gift cards." Keep in mind what Melinda Emerson said, "Promote with care." If you're selly and telly, you lose followers on all platforms. The key to social business is the "know, like, and trust factor." Once you've established a relationship of trust, you can gently open the door to a promotion opportunity.

I created and use the LEAP method in social media:

Listen
Engage
Appreciate
Praise

It works. Take a social leap!

Don't lead off by push-push-pushing out content. That opportunity to listen and to be gracious and to be apprecia-

tive attracts people to you, and that's how you work successfully in the social space.

Emerson, in *How to Become a Social Media Ninja*, says,
"Remember that social media marketing is a marathon, not
a sprint. You will get out of it what you invest in it and when
done right, you can expect to see what I call the 'triple ROI
of social media.'" The triple I's are: investment, influence,
identity. As she explains, your investment is your time. By
sharing content, small business owners build influence,
which can be monetized. Everything in social media is about
building your brand identity.

I don't claim to be a social media marketing expert. I
don't even claim to be a restaurant marketing expert. The
one true expertise I claim is recognizing experts! I've read
everything Melinda Emerson has published, have watched
her videos, read her blogs and other posts regularly, have par-
ticipated in her #SmallBizChat on Twitter (you should too,
it's a great, fast-paced way to spend an hour learning from
small business experts on Wednesday nights). I actively pay
attention to experts.

PICK YOUR SOCIAL PLATFORMS

The digital world is rapidly expanding. Apple launched the
AppStore in July 2008 with 800 apps. Back then, you could
find a couple of dozen apps in each category. There are now
millions of apps across multiple platforms from Apple to
Droid to Windows and across devices such as phones, tablets,

and netbooks. Every single day you can find something new. With all this expansion, social can feel really overwhelming, but it doesn't have to be.

Start easy, with Facebook. Get the hang of it. It's worth repeating: you've got to learn to walk before you can run! There are well over a billion people on Facebook. Today, if Facebook were a country, it would be the third largest in the world, after China and India, and it's on track to become "the largest country" by 2017. The people in your town, whether a tiny little place in Nebraska, New Zealand, or Nevada, or a big city in Canada, are on Facebook.

Your restaurant must be there too, interacting with guests and potential guests, listening to them, hearing and engaging relevantly. Start with Facebook; get good at it.

Set your restaurant page up the right way, as a business profile, not an individual profile. Add your menu, pictures, videos. With 1.13 trillion likes and 150 billion Facebook friend connections already, you've got no time to waste. Get ready to engage, and start by developing trust.

"You don't instantly have trust; it has to be earned," says Coach Mike Krzyzewski.

MONITORING YOUR ONLINE REPUTATION: REVIEW SITES

There are thousands of ways guests and others can talk about our business online. Keep in mind the first R of branding success: reputation. Build it and vigilantly monitor and maintain it.

Your job is to monitor to your best ability and be part of the conversation. Probably the site most restaurateurs are familiar with is Yelp! Whether you have ever visited Yelp! or not, your business is likely there. Go to Yelp! Enter your restaurant in the search box and claim your business. Do the same with Google, TripAdvisor, UrbanSpoon, FourSquare, and as many other places you can find reviews about your business. Set up Google Alerts so you can be notified when your company appears in reviews and comments and then respond appropriately in a timely manner.

EVERYONE'S A CRITIC

Sometimes you'll find a great review. They're going to say your service was fantastic, the food was outrageous, the place was fabulous, the bathrooms were superclean, the parking lot was nice, the signage helpful, everything was perfect—people raving about you.

You'll also find terrible reviews. The service sucked. Food was overpriced. The plate looked like vomit. The staff was a poor excuse for a person. People actually say things like this, and you don't know it if you're not monitoring it. What are Misty's three Rs of branding again?

Reputation management is modern marketing. Smart companies monitor the social web. Be smart.

Reputation, relationship, reliability. You must monitor your reputation. *Reputation management is modern marketing.* Smart companies monitor the social web. Be smart.

Here's what I love most about social media: You own it. You don't have to pay anybody for it. You are the media. You control the channels. You control the message. You're in charge.

RESPOND APPROPRIATELY

Every single public review of Squeeze In from the start of Yelp! until now has been responded to by either Shila or myself. We think it's that important.

Like attracts like, and negativity attracts more negativity. If you leave unflattering reviews unanswered, others will say, "Yes, I had that experience too! My plate looked like vomit! There were cockroaches and mice poops in the bathroom and a human skeleton sticking out of their dumpster!" It's shocking the things people will say and do behind the veil of anonymity. By not responding appropriately, you're allowing it.

We discovered when we very first started monitoring Yelp! in or around 2008 there was a negative vibe one person had started and other people glommed onto it. It was like fire getting out of control, and I began monitoring Yelp! weekly, responding to every single publicly posted review. Good or bad, it didn't matter, I responded. Shila took over responding in 2012.

I discovered responding quelled negativity immediately, as reviewers realized they couldn't just get on their bully pulpit unchecked. Some reviews are incredibly difficult to read. Yes, we're human beings, we make mistakes. We don't give the most excellent service every single time, regardless of how excellent our training is. Sometimes we fail. It happens. We apologize and we evolve.

Never ever fuel a fire. A great counselor, Jim Hershey once said, "If you can't make it better, don't make it worse." You can make it better. You choose.

You'll find some Yelp! reviews I have publicly responded to that say, "Dear Shawn C, I'm so sorry you had such a terrible experience in my restaurant. You can't believe how hard it was to personally read your review. I'm deeply disappointed and I apologize."

Then I'll go on to say publicly we may not cut the mustard every time, but we surely try. We've got systems, training, standards. I'll inform the reviewer, "I've already addressed your comment with our regional manager, general manager, kitchen manager, and all associates working at the time of your visit. I've expressed your concerns directly and personally. We're using your experience as a training opportunity. Thank you so much for putting your review online."

You might be personally crushed by the reviews—and, of course, thrilled with the glowing ones! Everyone else reading your reviews will know you are active and learning from criticism, valid or not and that you respond and appreciate praise as well. Battles? Don't fight your battles in public.

You will surely lose. You've surely heard: "Never do battle with people who buy ink by the barrel!" On the Internet, ink is *free!*

CAN PEOPLE FIND YOU ON THE INTERNET?

Pew Internet published the report, *Where People Get Information about Restaurants and Other Local Businesses.* A few pertinent findings are these:

People looking for information about local restaurants and other businesses say they rely on the Internet, especially search engines, ahead of any other source.

Newspapers, both printed copies and the websites of newspaper companies, run second behind the Internet as the source that people rely on for news and information about local businesses, including restaurants and bars.

And word of mouth, particularly among non-Internet users, is also an important source of information about local businesses.

People who seek out information and news about local businesses and restaurants are a diverse and somewhat upscale group. As distinct populations, they are more likely to live in relatively well-off households—those earning $75,000 or more—and have college educations.

In addition, the 55 percent of adults who get information about restaurants, bars, and clubs are more likely to be women, young adults, urban, and technology adopters.

DAILY DEAL SITES

Here's the quick and dirty: Run, don't walk, away from any organization that wants to sell your $100 gift certificate for $50 and you get $25. Just say no. Be smart. Build your own database. Create a herd of loyal followers through excellence and build an iron cage of loyalty around them. Go to my must-have book list at MistyYoung.com right now and click to pick up the most dog-eared book on my desk, Dan Kennedy's

> Run, don't walk, away from any organization that wants to sell your $100 gift certificate for $50 and you get $25.

Ultimate Marketing Plan. Use the checklists and resources in the back to build your own plan. Dan's the ultimate marketing expert. You're the expert in your restaurant. The book will be in your hands in two days and you can read it in one.

TWITTER

Today, there are 500 million Twitter accounts sending *400 million tweets daily.* This incredible "microblogging" social tool has matured from the "I'm brushing my teeth" tweets to the sophisticated and deep opportunity it now presents to integrate into your guest's lives. Setting up and using Twitter is easy: Create a Twitter account, using a name representative of your company. If your restaurant is the Sunset Diner, try to get your name as your "@handle." Ours is, of course,

@SqueezeIn. My personal account is @MistyYoung. I also tweet using the handle @Restaurant_Lady.

You might have to get creative. If your restaurant is Sunrise Cafe, I'm willing to bet you somebody else already has @SunriseCafe, so you might have to be @SunriseOmaha or @SunriseOttowa. Be creative, but also let people know who you are. Don't get clever; it doesn't help on Twitter. Being specific helps.

Search and follow people in your region. Let's say you're in Omaha. In Twitter, set up an account and search "Omaha." Now you're going to find people in Omaha on Twitter, and you can follow them.

Pay attention to their tweets (aka Twitter feed). Sounds like a strange phrase, but the definition is simple. All it means is taking a look at what they're posting, sending out to their network, the people who have subscribed to their messages. Much of this can be automated, using a free tool such as HootSuite, which I highly recommend.

General Twitter etiquette says if I follow you, you follow me back. It's not written in stone, it's thought of as a common courtesy.

Building a Twitter following isn't difficult: After geographics, search for and follow people writing about dinner, wine, barbeque, steak, lasagna, breakfast, whatever topics are most relevant to your business. The search ability in Twitter is amazing, and there are apps such as TweetAdder that help tremendously in searching and following users.

Much of building, editing, and maintaining an audience can even be automated.

We look for people who write about breakfast, about food, about Reno/Tahoe, or Truckee. We follow those people. Many tourists on their way into our town, say, "Headed to Reno this weekend. Wonder what I'm going to do?"

We're right there, tweeting these folks: "Glad you'll be @Reno this weekend. Stop by @SqueezeIn; here's our menu: [shortlink]." We do our best to use Twitter as an interactive, useful tool for visitors and other followers.

Twitter's a hugely valuable tool. Just do it!

PICTURES AND VIDEO, THE HEARTBEAT OF SOCIAL MEDIA

Photos and video must be a big component of your social space.

I've heard it said that 90 percent of web traffic will be video by 2014.

Here's a cool tactic: If there's a group at the Squeeze having a fun time, taking pictures, actively engaged, we've trained our associates to say, "Hey, would you like me to take a group picture or video for you?" They do not say, "So you can put it on Facebook. So you can tweet it. So you can put it on Pinterest."

We lovingly serve our guests in many ways. Helping them create, capture, and store their cherished memories for the long term is one of them. We never ask guests to post or share. Never. We just offer to help capture their media.

We know what people do with pictures and video: they post on Facebook, tweet, and pin. Helping our guests by taking photos and videos is one more tactic we deploy to receive earned media from our own guests, *our ambassadors.*

We also regularly share candid, real-time images of our associates. These are fun, in-the-moment images posted to our social sites.

According to Pinterest Insider, 57 percent of Pinterest users interact with *food-related content, which is the number-one content category on Pinterest!* Pinterest hit 10 million U.S. monthly unique visitors faster than any independent site in history, and the most popular age group on the site is 25 to 34 years old.

According to a psychographic analysis of members in our own EggHead Breakfast Club database, a segment of this age group, known as mixed singles, tracks the second overall highest individual spending per member, at $195.85, second only to "aging upscale" members at $202.59. Members of the mixed singles group have few children, are likely to be in school, and have lower income but spend like crazy at the Squeeze. Ronald Reagan was elected president while they were growing up listening to New Wave music and watching the premier of *Flashdance.* These people love to spend money. I want them in my restaurants!

Create a free Pinterest page to pin and repin pictures of food, beverages, associates, happy guests, and fun celebrations. Invite your guests to join you in the social theater. Phyllis Ann Marshall of FoodPower.com recently said, "They say a picture's worth a thousand words, but today, it could be worth a thousand dollars! If you're like us, you love looking at mouthwatering shots of food—so crisp and clear you can almost taste the flavors. Nothing drives traffic to restaurants more than hunger, so take advantage of every photo op to create cravings! YUM!! Got a great photo? Facebook it, Tweet it, Instagram it, Pin it ... whatever you do, share it with your network, and have them share it with theirs. That's how social networking works—your network is strengthened by your followers' networks! It's what creates a buzz and can propel your brand!" Smart.

WORD OF MOUTH IS NOW WORD OF MEDIA

Conventional wisdom says word of mouth is the best way to market a restaurant, right? Social media changes everything, morphing word of mouth to word of media. This is the new media. Don't take a dip; jump right into the social stream.

According to Nielsen's *State of the Media: The Social Media Report*, "Consumers frequently trust the recommendations of their peers, making social media an ideal platform for influencers to spread their ideas and purchase power. Research by NM Incite shows that

> Social media changes everything, morphing word of mouth to word of media. This is the new media. Don't take a dip; jump right into the social stream.

60 percent of social media users create reviews of products and services. In fact, consumer-created reviews/ratings are the preferred source for information about product/service value, price, and product quality."

Did you see that? *Consumer-created reviews/ratings are the preferred source.* When did that happen? It doesn't matter. What does is that you change your language now by adding a new phrase: Word of media—social media—and take immediate action to incorporate it into your marketing approach. Here's an easy strategy: make a free quick response (QR) code, those little pixelly, boxy-looking things (Google free QR code generator). Make the code link to a review website for your business. Have custom QR codes printed on table tents or small cards your servers can hand to thrilled guests to lead them to a review site in the moment. Right now. Thank them profusely for doing a review.

The world of communication is changing fast. How many times do you pick up the phone and call people? You don't. You text them, right? Many now text to ask, "Is it okay if I call you?" Marketing communications has transitioned out of analog life and into digital life, and we have to transition with it if we're to be successful.

YOUR WEBSITES

The days of not having a website are long over. You can have a website up *today*. It's not hard to do. If you don't know how to do it, stop dinking around with it and hire someone. In addition to a basic web presence, you've got to have a mobile website, where visitors arriving on a mobile device will automatically get detected and shifted to a clean, skinny, finger-friendly website.

FOURSQUARE

Foursquare is a cool tool. Guests check in at your restaurant. They come in, they sit down, and post, "Guess where I'm at? I'm at the Squeeze In. I'm the mayor of the Squeeze In."

What does that mean? It means they've checked in at your place more than anybody else. Have a special deal in place for them. The mayors of the Squeeze In get a free mimosa. If they don't drink booze, they get a free orange juice. We like to hook them up. We like to recognize their word of media. Using digital tools, we stay involved with our guests.

MODERN METHODS AND PUBLIC RELATIONS

When I left public relations in 2003 to buy the Squeeze In, the term social media didn't exist. In the 2002 book *The Anatomy of Buzz,* author Emanual Rosen calls the emerging social scene "invisible networks." He said, "Buzz is not about elegant advertising or glitzy trade shows. It's about what happens in the invisible networks—the interpersonal information networks that connect customers to each other.

It's about what customers—the people who pay money for products—tell each other about these products."

Even back then, at the dawn of this new age in communication, he said, "Invisible networks have always been important in the diffusion of certain products. Today they are critical and can no longer be ignored. In order to compete, companies must understand that they are not selling to individual customers but, rather, to networks of customers." How true. Describing the emerging tools on the net as electronic word of mouth, Rosen further says, "If these aggregated buzz tools take off, the importance of (product) quality will increase even more." Boy did they take off, and boy, was Rosen right!

The social media landscape has developed in just a few short years. You do not have to become an expert; you just have to take action, be involved. Defeat the restaurant killing FTI Syndrome with the only known treatment: action. Word of mouth/word of media is critical for your continued success. It's not too late now, but if you wait, it will be that much harder to catch the fast moving train.

With modern marketing through social media, you build your herd with individuals and their networks. It's a worthy approach to cultivate dedicated, interactive, engaged guests. Old-school public relations was about mass media. Do you even hear that term anymore? Not so much. What you hear is social media.

I said earlier it had been a dream of ours to own commercial real estate. While we're not there yet, we were smart enough to see the deep value of social real estate and we scooped it up. What are the top three rules in real estate? Location! Location! Location! And, in the case of social real estate locations, they're free! You are the media; you control your own media. *These are the most powerful free marketing resources ever available in the history of small businesses.*

Get your social media sites up and running and convert guests and potential guests one by one. It might sound overwhelming, but it's not. It just requires a diligent, focused approach. A billion people are on Facebook. They're in your town. They're in your churches and temples and places of worship. They're in the grocery store. They're looking for you. You've got to meet your guests and your potential guests where they are: in the social sphere.

You can do it. Ask questions. Go look around. Here's a four-letter word we haven't talked about yet: p-l-a-y. Go play.

You can't break the Internet, okay? Don't be afraid of it; make it work for you!

Invest one hour daily learning about social media and then remember the key: You own that media real estate. You're the broadcaster, the journalist; you control the message. You attract the audience to you by listening, engaging, and appreciating, praising, and interacting with them. Be attractive! Leap!

INGREDIENTS FOR SUCCESS

1. Post on your wall, "Marketing is Math." Get your emotions out of the way.
2. Set up three free social media accounts and start using them.
3. Memorize Misty's three Rs of branding success: reputation; relationship; reliability. Be reliable.
4. Listen to understand not to make a point.
5. Monitor your online reviews and respond appropriately. Never ever fuel a fire.
6. Serve your guests by helping them capture memories and media through mobile devices.
7. Ask for reviews from happy guests. Use QR codes to make it easy for them.
8. Own social media real estate. It's valuable and it's free!

CHAPTER TEN

The Secret Recipe

THE SECRET RECIPE

Ingredients

- love
- action
- gratitude
- leadership

Method

Fold equal parts love and action until well blended with a light, bubbly texture. Mix in gratitude and leadership until consistency of warm happiness. Bake in custom 98.6 degree oven. This dish never finishes baking; it may need to be turned or fluffed occasionally during process. Enjoy warm and share abundantly with others!

Chef note: as long as the ingredients are in good supply, this dish, although in high demand, never runs out.

In the decade since I've owned the Squeeze In, I've responded to thousands of people in person, and through e-mails, and phone calls. I've given generously of my time in meetings and "pick-your-brain" sessions and spoken to groups of independent restaurant owners all over the country, eager to know exactly what we did and how we did it. You've now heard the entire story from top to bottom. You know exactly what we did and how we did it. And, you have the secret recipe.

I've loved sharing my experiences over these years, but I realized how much more effective I could be if I were to do as Dan Kennedy suggests and systematize the "one thing you do over and over"—hence, the book in your hands. In this book I've answered the questions I've been asked constantly from other restaurateurs and the media. My purpose is to help you grow and prosper. I can pour myself and my experiences into more independent restaurant owners with the tools available through modern media, and I'm eager to do so. I want to add value to you and help you succeed.

I hope you've found useful tools and information in these pages. As you now readily understand—and thank you for reading my story—I am all about finding and sharing answers and serving others.

It has been my goal to share my story in a meaningful and relevant way to demonstrate the power of love, the value of asking and answering questions, the intelligence of planning and action, and of course to share my discovery, the Five Irrefutable Laws of Restaurant Success. If you apply what you've learned in this book, and furthermore, follow the many leads and free resources available at the website, you'll be better positioned in your restaurant success journey. You have surely seen that the most basic ingredients in the secret recipe are *love folded in with action*. I love success. I love controlling my own time. I love serving others, including you.

I love the energy you have shared with me in reading this book and would love to hear you've been able to overcome FTI syndrome, and that you've implemented the principles here into your restaurant to benefit yourself, your family, associates, and community. I hope you'll find an opportunity to share the message here with other independent restaurateurs. We can and should help each other; there's plenty of business to go around.

Professionalizing your restaurant doesn't have to be overwhelming. We can hack into the fast track of success by modeling those at the pinnacle of profitability and by systematizing our businesses. Success comes in part from using systems every day. It's not easy to systematize every aspect of your business, but it's worth every moment.

One of the amazing benefits for me in having developed the Squeeze In as the well-known brand it is today is that it has attracted a lot of attention.

It's attracted the attention of the *New York Times*, America Online, AOL.com's *Daily Finance*, *National Geographic World*, the *San Francisco Chronicle*, the *Reno Gazette-Journal*, *Independent Restaurateur Magazine*, *Powder* and *Sunset* magazines, and way too many more to list. It's attracted the attention of blogs and television and magazines and restaurant experts and owners.

And you already know it attracted the Food Network and Bobby Flay's attention.

He came in from the blizzard that morning and we were ready to meet the challenge. We had been prepping for success and it showed. We had spent years gearing up, developing our website and systems, making the upgrades, developing a loyal brand. When the Food Network asked the questions, we were ready with answers immediately.

We had followed the learning path to personal growth and development. We stayed focused on love and improvement through education in college, politics, and the spiritual journey. We followed our dreams with enthusiasm and energy. We said, "So what?" to the past so we could move forward from rags to restaurants despite the odds against us.

We stayed focused on our love and happiness while raising kids and giving generously. We strove to be kind and courteous, teaching our daughters to do the same in a world full of lovers and others.

We asked question after question, implemented everything we learned, and deeply explored failure and success as we grew the company from one location to four. We continued our devotion to learning and discovered the Five Irrefutable Laws of Restaurant Success as we developed our leadership and our brand.

You've heard about how much action we've taken, which is the antidote to the poisonous FTI syndrome and the absolute key to our planning and strength. We never stopped refining, understanding all the while the value in daily development and the compound nature of it over time. We implemented a marketing and loyalty system that has paid handsomely. We get what we settle for and we've continued to question, question, question through it all.

As we became more sophisticated in our operations and financials, we hacked success on the fast track and began to understand and prioritize at an even deeper level.

You saw how we shifted from processes to people, making not only our guests, but our associates the center of our attention, and you saw how everything transformed. Through mission statements, checking the checker, comprehensive training, guest surveys, our Format program, we replicated ourselves to extend our reach and allowed for no wiggle room in our approach to quality. We develop happy associates to help create happy guests and verify it all through guest experience management and system wide review.

We value our associates, our guests, each other and our businesses while serving our communities with kindness. We give our guests a no-risk guarantee and when things go wrong, we apologize, evolve, and keep loving them and enlisting them in creative ways to help us build more restaurants. We ask them to refer guests to us and thank them immensely for doing so.

You've seen the importance we place on marketing, math, and making social media work through numerous interactive platforms. You've seen our emphasis on photos and videos and modern media.

Our path has taken us through strategy, tactics, accountability and results and led us to the Five Irrefutable Laws of Restaurant Success. We fell in love with the Squeeze In and then nurtured, served, and protected it as it grew.

I've enjoyed working to spread the message of love for your healthy business and self and reiterate again our goal is to fall back in love with our businesses in a structured, focused, intentional way.

At the end of the day my message is your restaurant is a business first, standing on a foundation of operations and financials, measurement and analytics. All these topics have helped make my company successful and helped me become an independent restaurant coach and consultant known as the Restaurant Lady.

I've mentioned my active involvement as a member of Rory Fatt's mastermind group. This is a very valuable way I choose to spend my time. I visit with other successful restaurant owners interested in working *on* their businesses and regularly present on the national stage about training, marketing, accountability, and leadership, and I share stories about experiences in my own restaurant. I write a guest column monthly for Rory's restaurant industry newsletter and get to serve my restaurant colleagues by adding value to their businesses. All of this makes me happy. I like being happy.

I've been a guest speaker in cities all over the country, New York, Philadelphia, Chicago, Washington D.C., Phoenix, Vancouver BC, at conferences and special events, from regional chapters of the American Marketing Association and Public Relations Society of America to crowdfunding events and many others. I was invited to the White House to participate as a small business representative in the discussion on national health-care reform.

Recently, Pitney Bowes and Google hosted a live-streamed media event in New York City to discuss modern marketing techniques. I was recruited and thrilled to serve as one of only four panelists and to be the anchor speaker at an exclusive luncheon.

What attracted the event sponsor to me was my focus, my healthy obsession with the numbers. I love how using analytics and metrics drive success through monitoring, adjusting, and accountability. The esteemed panel included Jeff Crouse, national vice president of Pitney Bowes, Melinda Emerson of the *New York Times,* recognized as the number-one small business expert by Forbes, and also Tim Freeth of Google. Yeah, I got to serve on *that* panel. It was cool. I love public speaking and you already know I love being in the media spotlight!

I'm honored to add value in so many ways to my small business colleagues. We're in the trenches together, each of us developing our leadership daily to serve our families, our associates and guests, and meet our goals through our businesses. What an honor and privilege!

As you now know, at the Squeeze In, we do a tremendous amount of healthy analysis—and appropriate adjusting. I think that's what really set us apart and what sets me apart as a business leader. We look at the numbers continuously, obsessively, relentlessly. What do we do with that information? We feed it back into the system for constant refinement.

This number crunching and feedback is something of particular interest when I talk to local business associations, no matter what business their members are in. It isn't just about restaurants. Numbers are the universal language translating into every business from restaurants to retail and everything in between.

People have long been coming to me for answers, and I am happy to help as an expert, coach and leadership developer. It's why Bobby Flay came to me to learn how an omelette becomes one of the "Best Omelettes on the Planet."

And now, I stand ready to serve you.

What's the biggest room in the world? The room for improvement. Step inside with me; I've been here for years!

You know that feeling when you're falling in love, that tickle in your tummy, that excitement, that spring in your step. You've experienced that fantastic feeling and can remember the day you opened your restaurant, or purchased it, or set foot in it for the first time. You can focus on that feeling and have it back again if you choose. Be intentional.

In addition to the prime question, "what does success look like to me?" I'm always focused on my personal ultimate questions: How may I serve? What is my truth? I ask these fundamental questions of myself in all areas and have found the ultimate answers, love and action, gratitude and leadership.

Love for my spirit to seek guidance and focused contemplation. Love for my body and family to seek health. Love for my business and community to seek success. *Love, kindness, compassion, and courtesy for others, to offer help and to be of service.* I am thankful for the opportunity to have graduated from college, healing school, be a Certified John Maxwell Team Member and to have delivered and attended many business programs, workshops, and presentations. I am truly blessed.

Over the course of time, I have come to realize each of us, in our being human, has a different truth. That truth is not the same for everyone. But there is a common denominator: *the truth continuum for all humans is the same, completely identical.* It looks like a standard bell curve.

In the center, at the tall point, stands our own individual truth, our light. At the corresponding edges, both left and right, are the standard deviations from our truth. Off center is where we humans find problems. I have found when I am standing, centered in my truth, I am in harmony, no discord. Standing to the left or the right of my truth, varying my solidity in any way, I am in discordance. The further I move from center, the more discord, the more chaos. *The same is true for you. This is the human condition without fail.* Only your personal truth varies. We feel like imposters and frauds when we stray from our own individual truth.

What is your truth? Stand in it. The closer you stand to the center of your truth, the higher your vibrational frequency, the stronger your signal, which weakens upon your deviation.

> What is your truth? Stand in it. The closer you stand to the center of your truth, the higher your vibrational frequency, the stronger your signal, which weakens upon your deviation. At the center, you feel buoyant, light, energized, whole.

At the center, you feel buoyant, light, energized, whole. You love the universe. You love others and are loved in return. You are attracted to service, which itself is also attractive. Be attractive.

Albert Einstein said, "The most important question a person can ask is: 'Is the Universe a friendly place?'" We must each answer that for ourselves, but choosing a "yes" answer helps attract and deliver success through the secret recipe. You decide.

Don't deny yourself, your family and loved ones, your friends, business associates, your guests, and community of the best you there is. Stand in your truth, ready, eager, and able to give of your best and highest self.

You don't have to be perfect. You just have to take action. Remember the recipe method is: Fold equal parts love and action until well blended with a light, bubbly texture. Mix in gratitude and leadership until consistency of warm happiness. Bake in custom 98.6 degree oven. This dish never finishes baking, it may need to be turned or fluffed occasionally during process. Enjoy warm and share abundantly with others!

Nothing happens until something moves. You've got to start moving. Reading a book isn't enough. You must now act. You will stumble. You might even fall. You may burn the edges a bit. It's all good. Start mixing, baking, and serving.

Step into your truth and make it happen!

With love,

Misty Young
The Restaurant Lady

How can you use this book?

MOTIVATE

EDUCATE

THANK

INSPIRE

PROMOTE

CONNECT

Why have a custom version of *From Rags to Restaurants?*

- Build personal bonds with customers, prospects, employees, donors, and key constituencies
- Develop a long-lasting reminder of your event, milestone, or celebration
- Provide a keepsake that inspires change in behavior and change in lives
- Deliver the ultimate "thank you" gift that remains on coffee tables and bookshelves
- Generate the "wow" factor

Books are thoughtful gifts that provide a genuine sentiment that other promotional items cannot express. They promote employee discussions and interaction, reinforce an event's meaning or location, and they make a lasting impression. Use your book to say "Thank You" and show people that you care.

CPSIA information can be obtained at www.ICGtesting.com
Printed in the USA
BVOW022245140713

325653BV00006B/10/P

9 781599 323770